Callaghan, Denis

Allan Watson

HODDER
GIBSON
PART OF HACHETTE LIVRE UK

Y700

The Publishers would like to thank the following for permission to reproduce copyright material:

Photo credits Please see List of Illustrations for photo acknowledgements

Every effort has been made to trace all copyright holders, but if any have been inadvertently overlooked the Publishers will be pleased to make the necessary arrangements at the first opportunity.

Although every effort has been made to ensure that website addresses are correct at time of going to press, Hodder Gibson cannot be held responsible for the content of any website mentioned in this book. It is sometimes possible to find a relocated web page by typing in the address of the home page for a website in the URL window of your browser.

Hachette's policy is to use papers that are natural, renewable and recyclable products and made from wood grown in sustainable forests. The logging and manufacturing processes are expected to conform to the environmental regulations of the country of origin.

Orders: please contact Bookpoint Ltd, 130 Milton Park, Abingdon, Oxon OX14 4SB. Telephone: (44) 01235 827720. Fax: (44) 01235 400454. Lines are open 9.00 – 5.00, Monday to Saturday, with a 24-hour message answering service. Visit our website at www.hoddereducation.co.uk. Hodder Gibson can be contacted direct on: Tel: 0141 848 1609; Fax: 0141 889 6315; email: hoddergibson@hodder.co.uk

© Denis Callaghan and Allan Watson 2008
First published in 2008 by
Hodder Gibson, an imprint of Hodder Education,
Part of Hachette Livre UK,
2a Christie Street
Paisley PA1 1NB

Impression number   5 4 3 2 1
Year   2012 2011 2010 2009 2008

Cover photo © SMK Foto/Statens Museum for Kunst, Copenhagen (top), © Lalique corsage Calouste Gulbenkian Foundation (bottom)
Typeset in ScalaSans 10 point by DC Graphic Design Limited
Printed in Italy

A catalogue record for this title is available from the British Library

ISBN-13: 978 0 340 92809 7

Contents

Introduction

This book deals with the Art and Design Studies element of Art and Design Higher and Intermediate 2 courses. In particular, it is geared towards preparing you for the external exam.

As you will know, Higher and Intermediate Art and Design courses involve the study of three units: Expressive, Design and Art and Design Studies. Expressive and Design units are assessed at the end of the course through the submission of a portfolio of practical work which will be marked by SQA examiners. Art and Design Studies, however, is assessed during the examination diet by a formal question paper set by the SQA. This question paper has two sections, one covering Art Studies (Expressive) and the other Design.

Throughout your course you will learn about artists and designers relevant to the units of study you are following. That is, if you are studying Still Life for your practical folio, you should be studying the work of significant Still Life artists who have been active during the period 1750 to the present. Likewise, if your practical Design folio is Jewellery, you will study prominent jewellery designers from the same period. On occasion, artists or designers active before 1750 are mentioned in this text, but only for purposes of introducing the theme. They **should not** be used as examples of practice within your examination.

The study of artists and designers associated with your practical work should help inform and assist you in developing your own ideas and techniques and improve your practical performance. Your personal research should also provide you with the evidence to complete your Art and Design Study.

Later in this introduction you will find general advice on essay writing and answering the sort of questions you are likely to come across in the examination paper. This advice can be used no matter what your subject focus is. The rest of the book is divided into two main sections, the first focusing on Art Studies, and the second covering Design. Each section contains chapters that discuss the associated topic areas e.g. portraiture, fashion or graphic design. At the end of the book you will also find a brief description of each of the movements explored within all subject areas to use as a reference.

Included in each chapter is discussion on prominent artists, designers and movements associated with the topic area. **The information given on artists, designers and movements is not exhaustive and should only be seen as a basis for further in-depth study.** The examples used are just that – examples. You may know of or prefer others. Try to make your study personal: if you care about the topic, you will become more involved and as a result gain more benefit.

Each chapter also includes sample questions and answers you may be faced with in your exam. The marks they would achieve are indicated and a comment on their strengths or weakness is included. You should try to read the comments closely and understand how the answers achieved the mark. This will help you stay focused when answering practice questions. Reading some of the sample answers from sections other than the ones you are studying should also assist your understanding of the standards required.

Included in each chapter are a number of activities for you to complete. Some of them are set in order to give you practice at developing your critical skills; others test your knowledge and understanding of the work of artists and designers you are interested in. If you complete the activities and are thorough in your preparation, you will prepare yourself well for the final exam.

The Art and Design Studies Examination

There are two sections to the question paper at both Higher and Intermediate 2 and you must answer one full question from each section.

The examination at Higher level is one and a half hours long. In that time you have to answer two full questions, each of which will have a Part A and Part B. At Intermediate 2 the examination is one hour long and you also have two full questions, each of which will have a Part A and B, to answer.

Part A of each question at Higher is worth 10 marks and Part B is worth 20 marks. At Higher level, a good rough plan is to give 15 minutes to the Part A answer and 30 minutes to the Part B answer of each question. At Intermediate 2, Parts A and B of each question are worth 10 marks so you should give roughly 15 minutes to each answer.

> **TIP**
>
> - *Make sure that you choose artists or designers from different time periods. This is not required for Intermediate 2 but it is still a good idea to know artists and designers from different periods, movements or styles.*
> - *Know the nationality of the artists or designer and when they worked.*
> - *Know the movement or style they are associated with and what influenced them.*
> - *Always refer to two artists or designers.*
> - *Do not try more than one full question from each section.*

The questions set for this exam relate to six major themes of visual arts and six major areas of design most commonly studied in schools for the practical work and coursework. These are:

- Portraiture
- Figure Composition
- Still Life
- Natural Environment
- Built Environment
- Fantasy and Imagination

- Graphic Design
- Product Design
- Interior Design
- Environmental and Architectural Design
- Jewellery Design
- Fashion and Textile Design

You should try to make connections between your chosen theme or design area and your practical work in the course. Art and Design Studies should be an opportunity to deepen and broaden your knowledge of the areas of visual art and design that really interest you.

Seeing and studying original works is important to your development in Art and Design. Whichever theme you elect to study for the Expressive Activity, you should use your sketchbook to collect things that interest you in other artists' work. Surround yourself with your favourite figure compositions, still lifes etc. Find out about the methods of the artists that interest you and practise them. You will find that your own art work improves from the knowledge you have gained through your research on other artists. Keep a notebook or scrapbook with examples of artists' work and write down personal notes about the things that move you, thrill you and inspire you.

THEMES IN VISUAL ART

Themes are the contexts in which artists work. Some universal themes have always attracted artists. The reason for this is that artists like to express ideas about the human condition. Love, beauty, conflict, drama, identity and political and social issues have always inspired artists to work in the six visual art themes of the course. Visual artists are informed by their personal responses to themes that really motivate them.

In Art Studies you can choose to study from six of the most universal themes that have attracted these artists. You can also choose to study one or more of these themes in the practical work for your course. The advantage in this approach is that the different themes, for example still life and portraiture, will influence one another in the practical work as well as coursework.

The sections in this book on each topic area will provide you with specific information about the different themes, as well as provide a broad overview of their development over time.

PART A QUESTIONS

In this part of the examination you need to critically evaluate selected unseen examples of visual art and design. This should not be new to you as much of what you have learned in previous years will have prepared you for critical evaluation.

In Art Studies you have to critically evaluate the use of identified visual elements and media, methods, aspects of art practice and aspects of communication. This last element will include mood, atmosphere, thoughts, feelings, ideas and meaning in the selected example from your personal viewpoint. Well-reasoned and justified personal opinions and responses to the work are required at this level. At Higher, you should have a well-developed critical vocabulary, made up of relevant art terms. You should avoid only telling the 'story' of the work, rather respond by analysing the example and commenting critically on how the visual elements, media and materials have been used to achieve the artist's intentions and or meaning.

In Design Studies you have to critically evaluate identified aspects of design practise and issues. This will include elements such as style, communication, form, function, technology and ergonomics, in addition to the methods and materials used to achieve them. As with the examples of visual art, reasoned and justified personal opinion and responses to the work are required at Higher level.

Each area of design has a slightly different emphasis. There are differences in the design practice and issues considered by a fashion designer, for instance, than an architect. If you have studied architecture, then you should critically evaluate examples in terms of design concepts specific to architecture like the use of space, materials, form and function and aesthetics. In questions set for product design the emphasis is likely to be on design issues such as function and fitness for purpose, safety and ergonomics. In questions on textile and fashion design, there will be greater emphasis on the use of visual elements such as colour, shape and texture, as well as how the designer produces for a target market and the sources of inspiration that the designer has looked at.

PART B QUESTIONS

In this part of the exam you have to show knowledge and understanding acquired in your Art and Design Studies. A range of open-ended questions is set to reflect the major areas which you will have been exploring in your practical work for the course.

Part B questions are also set to assess your historical knowledge and understanding of the areas in visual arts and design. At Higher, you **must** include historical knowledge. When you study any important artist there will always be an historical trace. You must know what influenced your chosen artists and the influence that they had on others that followed. Artists influence each other, and throughout history have joined up with similar-minded artists to form movements such as the Impressionists and the Surrealists.

You must have knowledge of at least one area of the visual arts and one area of design or architecture. This should not be a problem when you study popular areas that are historically different such as Romanticism and Realism, or Art Nouveau and Bauhaus.

If you have chosen areas that are close together in time, make sure that you understand the differences between them. It is more difficult when the selected areas of the visual arts and design are chosen because of differences in style. These should be sufficiently contrasting to allow you to demonstrate an in-depth knowledge of your selected area and provide enough information to convince the marker that your studies have been well researched and your arguments well justified.

Essay Writing

The structure of either question can usually be answered along lines familiar to you from your other subjects. It is best to think of your essay as having three parts:

● Introduction

● Middle

● Conclusion

In your introduction you should make it clear to the marker that you understand what the question is asking you to do. You can do this by rephrasing the question as a statement and including the artists, designers or movements you plan to discuss. In this way you introduce the marker to the focus of your writing. Use the wording of the question to give a brief outline of what you intend to discuss in the middle section of your essay.

EXAMPLE

Two examples of designers from two different periods are Alphonse Mucha and Herbert Beyer. Mucha is associated with the Art Nouveau period which lasted from about 1890 to 1910. The movement began in Belgium and quickly spread to become an international style. Art Nouveau was a highly decorative style, influenced by nature.

Hebert Bayer worked at the Bauhaus school of design in Weimar, Germany. In contrast to Art Nouveau, Bauhaus designers believed in creating with the help of the machine. Both designers had very different approaches and ideas about graphic design.

By comparing the ideas and approaches of each designer, I am going to show how each made an important contribution to the development of graphic design.

The middle section is the longest part of your essay where you discuss your selected artists or designers in detail and analyse examples of their work to support your discussion. This is where you will be likely to pick up the most marks for showing your understanding of the movements and styles to which the artists or designers belong. In this section you can analyse examples of the work of artists and designers making sure that you always address the main points in the question about working methods, approaches and influences. In this section you can also:

● Use some biographical knowledge, briefly

● Write about the characteristics of your selected artist's or designer's work and of the movement and/or style they belong to

● Write about the approaches used by the artists or designers, including the materials, media and methods they use

● Analyse specific examples of the artist's or designer's work.

Finally, a conclusion can be used to draw together the ideas that you have discussed in the main body of the essay and explain why your artist or designer was important. If you have selected historically important artists or designers you will have knowledge of why they were important in their areas of design or movement in the visual arts.

Take a look at the following example to see how the three-part essay structure can help you.

EXAMPLE

Make clear in the introduction that you understand what the question is asking you to do. Use the wording of the question to give a brief outline of what you intend to discuss in the middle section of your essay.

Before the Industrial Revolution, many people designed and made their own products from the idea right through to the finished product. If it was something that lots of people needed then local craftsmen could be employed to make the object. The Industrial Revolution changed this and gave rise to factories, mechanised methods of manufacture. This led to the mass-production of products for the benefit of people. I am going to discuss the kettle and the evolution of its design.

The Bauhaus School of Design started in Germany after the First World War. They believed that design should be functional and made of honest, simple materials which emphasised their function.

Use the middle section of the essay to discuss your selected artists or designers in detail and analyse examples of their work to support your points.

The first design is by Marianne Brandt and was designed in 1924. The kettle is an example of Bauhaus Design. The second design is the cordless kettle. Both designs were created in response to user needs. Brandt's kettle was designed to be mass manufactured with stainless steel. The Seymour kettle was designed to include considerations of user needs and function.

Brandt's kettle is made from brass. The purpose of the Bauhaus design was to use simple materials to create individual style. This is especially achieved within this kettle where Brandt uses simple designs to create a stylish simple kettle which is almost ornamental rather than practical. The kettle is made from brass which might make it dangerous to use and would take time as it would have to be boiled on a stove. This would not be practical in today's society where speed and ease of use are a concern for the user.

The second kettle design is Seymour and Powell's cordless kettle of 1984. This was a revolutionary design cutting the number of steps taken to boil a kettle. The electric kettle was a big advance over the stove-mounted one. It didn't need a source of heat to make it work and it stayed clean and ready for use. This kettle added another feature to improve on existing kettles. It was cordless. The designers solved a major safety issue of an exposed power cable. By adding a power base they made the kettle easier to use.

TIP

Don't be too narrative and tell only the story of the selected examples of work. Think about the relevance of what you are writing to the question. When you are writing about individual works the critical evaluation skills that you use in Part A answers can be used to analyse individual examples.

Your conclusion should be at least a paragraph long. This is where you draw together the discussion that you have presented in the main body of the essay. You need to include comments about the importance of your selected artists or designers.

The electric cordless kettle was important because it was a big advance over anything that had come before. It didn't need a source of heat to make it work and it stayed clean and ready for use at a moment's notice. There was no exposed power cable making it safer than previous kettles. The cordless kettle is still in use today in many different varieties of styles.

Bauhaus design was important because it changed the way people thought about design and had a lasting influence on how we produce functional design with inexpensive mass-produced materials and machine processes.

Looking at Visual Art Works

In the examination for Art and Design studies you are expected to write about works that you may never have seen before as well as those you have studied in class. It is useful to have a strategy to help you structure how you look at works. If you do not have some basic strategy or plan for what you are looking at, it is very difficult to respond to an unseen work of art and design.

Some art works can arouse strong negative feelings. This should not put you off. People have always had positive and negative responses to works of visual art. However, it is not sufficient just to say 'I do not like this work' or 'I think this is horrible'.

Start your analysis with some very basic questions:

● How do I react to this work?

● Why does it make me feel or think like this?

● Does it make me think of other things I have seen?

● What does it remind me of?

● Why does it remind me of this?

Already, a whole range of different possible answers are there to steer you away from dead-end types of comments and toward engagement with the work.

Asking some basic questions of the work in front of you immediately allows you to start looking and thinking at the same time. Many of the mature artists that you will encounter have strong personal feelings and values that they wish to express in their works. These are not always the accepted values of the society or the age in which they lived. Visual artists have been deliberately rebellious and have often provoked controversy. Some, like the nineteenth century French artist Gustave Courbet, have even been imprisoned for the political beliefs that they expressed in their art.

It is also natural to ask yourself the question: 'What is this work about?' Asking this raises many more questions about what actually informed the artist when he/she conceived the work that you are looking at. Just like you, mature artists have a wide range of personal, social, political, emotional and cultural life experiences that inform how they think about their compositions. Each artist is an individual and over their careers they develop their own personal style, ways of using the media that they like most and the materials and techniques that are best suited to what they want to express. Artists express values that are personal to them. When you examine artwork that you have never seen before the exam, each element you identify is a clue to unravelling what the artist is expressing.

Asking what the work is about allows you to go on to pose another question: 'How did the artist create this work?' It may help to break this question down even further to help you with your analysis. A useful way of approaching this is to consider four basic standpoints that you can apply to virtually any new and unseen work. These are: Content, Form, Process and Mood. This approach to examining art was advocated by Rod Taylor in his books *Educating for Art: Critical Responses and Development* (1986) and *Understanding and Investigating Art* (1999).

CONTENT – LOOKING AT THE SUBJECT OF THE VISUAL ART WORK

The first standpoint to ask questions about is Content. When considering content, focus on the *subject* of the work in front of you.

- What is the subject matter? What is the work about? What is happening in it?

- What does the work represent? The subject may be very clear or hidden, using symbols or metaphors to point to other meanings or messages.

- What is the artist trying to say? A work of art, particularly figure composition, may tell a story. It may express a viewpoint about the artist's social, political, personal or moral views. It may represent strong values, ideas and religious beliefs. The title of a work often gives an indication of the artist's intentions and may influence the way you view the work.

- Is the work the product of direct observation or invented and imagined? Knowing whether the work is realistic, abstract, exaggerated or distorted also gives you clues to the intention of the artist who created it and allows you to think about why he or she chose a particular approach.

FORM – LOOKING AT THE VISUAL ELEMENTS

The second standpoint to ask questions about is Form. This allows you to pose and answer questions about how well the artist has used the various visual and composition elements of line, tone, colour, shape, pattern, texture and composition.

- How is the work composed?

- Is it balanced, diagonal?

- How has colour been used?

- Is it harmonious? Is it strongly contrasting, vivid, subtle, sad or happy?

- Are there recurring shapes?

- Does the work have a variety of texture?

- Are there recurring lines and rhythms in the work?

PROCESS – HOW THE WORK HAS BEEN DEVELOPED AND MADE

The third standpoint is Process and allows you to pose and answer questions about how the work might have been developed and produced, and the effectiveness of the techniques and processes used by the artist to achieve the success of the work. This involves thinking about and asking questions such as:

● How was the work made?

● What materials, tools, processes and techniques has the artist used?

● What kind of skills did the artist have?

● Does it look as if it was done quickly or over a long period of time?

MOOD – LOOKING AT THE COMMUNICATION OF MOODS AND FEELINGS

The fourth standpoint is Mood. This allows you to pose and answer other questions about the emotional qualities of the unseen work and how it may be received by a viewer. Ask questions such as:

● How do I react to this work?

● Is it disturbing, soothing, relaxing, happy or sad, provocative or challenging?

● Does it convey a mood?

● Does it have atmosphere?

● What were the artist's feelings when he or she produced this work?

● How does the work make me feel and why do I feel this way when I look at it?

The list of questions under each standpoint is not exhaustive. There will be others that you can think of on your own. The important thing is that you have a strategy for analysing any new and unseen work of art. Posing questions like this lets you consider your own reaction and response to the work while also considering its technical elements.

Now you have a basic strategy for looking at new and unseen works!

When you are analysing works in the Part B questions, it is helpful to know something of the wider historical context for your selected examples:

● When was it made? Knowing when the work was created can help you to understand why it was created.

● Where was it made? Who made it? The conditions of the period can have an effect on how the artist approached the task.

● Who was the work made for? Knowing the kind of person or group who commissioned the work can also help with your understanding of why it was made.

● What do you know about the artist and his or her life? The life of an artist shapes the work that he or she produces.

● What do you know about the movement or period to which he or she belonged? Knowledge of movements will deepen your understanding of the artists that you study.

TIP

For the Art and Design Studies examination you need to add opinion to this way of responding to unseen art works. It is easy to simply write 'I like' or 'I do not like' something. Justifying an opinion by giving reasons is a better way of expressing an opinion.

- Does the work relate to the social or political history of the period?

- Is the style/subject of the work related to works by other artists of the period?

- What is the format of the work? The size of the work and where it was intended to be viewed all contribute to the overall effect of an art work.

With any question you should look for a structure to your answer in the question itself. If you are asked to discuss methods, approaches and sources, for example, you have a clear lead into the discussion. Pause for a moment and list the number of things you could discuss in detail.

Read through the example below. By using the four standpoints discussed earlier, this example shows how the question could be handled in relation to fantasy and imagination. After the list was created, the response was broken down into paragraphs addressing each standpoint with an additional paragraph for opinion.

TIP

When you are writing about examples of the work of artists in Part B questions remember to include historical context.

EXAMPLE

Content	Dreams, juxtaposition, transformation distortion
Form	Composition, colour, shape and tone
Process	Realism, smooth brushstrokes
Mood	Eerie, nightmarish, sinister, disturbing

Form

You can see clearly that Dali has tried to give this work the appearance of a dream as everything looks out of place, just like dreams.◄ As in dreams, very unlikely things appear very real. Places and objects can change, so the whole effect is one of distortion.◄ Dali changes the setting scale of familiar objects and transforms them by making them (the timepieces) appear to melt. ◄

Odd changes in scale and perspective are also present and the sea appears to be on two different levels.◄ Odd juxtapositions are used like the insects crawling over the back of the watch as if it were rotting flesh.◄

Another odd distortion is in the folding fleshy creature in the centre of the picture. It appears to be a combination of different human and animal forms.◄

(◄ indicates a point worthy of 1 mark)

Now try this...

Read through the rest of this example with a classmate. Decide where you would award marks.

Content

My interpretation of this work is that it represents a distorted fantasy dream. The watches appear to have gone limp and the insects seem to be eating away at time. The very odd creature at the centre of the picture adds more confusion to it as it is difficult for the viewer to make out what it is. All of this makes me think that the work is a message about time and dreams. In my opinion this could be

Now try this, continued...

about the end of time as the landscape gives the impression of being remote and desolate and it is a place where time has stopped or is melting away.

Process

The whole landscape is bathed in an unnatural light. Dali uses very fine brushwork throughout the painting. By using meticulous photographic realism, dreams often appear very realistic. The use of colour also adds to the strangeness of the image and Dali's strong shadows help to create mystery.

Mood

Personally, I find this work very disturbing. The atmosphere created by the artist is sinister and threatening. Just as in a terrifying nightmare the work gives you the feeling of wanting to wake up to end the nightmare, but as time has stopped you are trapped forever.

Opinion

I really like this work. The idea of creating art from images of the subconscious mind appeals to me. The very precise realism used by Dali makes it seem as if you could enter this dream-like landscape.

Practise these techniques and ways of approaching art and design works as much as possible in preparing for your exam. That way, when you come to sit the exam you will feel more comfortable and secure in answering Part A and B questions on works you may never have seen before.

The illustrations used throughout this book are given as examples to help you understand the text. When it comes to attempting your own analysis of a particular piece of art shown in this book, it will be beneficial to look up larger versions of these illustrations to make sure that you gain as full an appreciation of the detail as possible.

Art Studies

Why Write about Art and Design?

Go into any of our leading bookshops or libraries and you will find large sections devoted to books on art and design. From the earliest times we have written down our thoughts about the work of artists, designers and architects. Ancient Greeks and Romans began to write about art to inform people about the meaning and purpose of art in our lives. By the time of the great Italian Renaissance, when artists such as Leonardo Da Vinci and Michelangelo flourished, writing about art had developed into a branch of history. This branch was called Art History.

Writers on art history have always sought to document the lives of artists and their works and to raise the status of artists so that their work is preserved for future generations to enjoy. As this discipline has developed, art historians have expanded their scope of writing to include the interpretation of art and making judgements about the quality and historical significance of the work that artists produce. Because art history covers many centuries, they also often explore the influences that artists (from the past and contemporaries) have had on each other. The subject of Art History has been taught by professors at universities all over Europe since the eighteenth century.

Today, Art and Design History are offered as degree courses at many universities and art colleges in Britain, Europe and America. You can even specialise in different historical periods (Neoclassicism, Eighteenth Century Art) or the history of art where you can concentrate on different movements or styles (Impressionism, Romanticism, Art Deco) in art and design.

The rise of the popular press in newspapers and magazines has also provided the opportunity for another form of writing about art to take place. This is art criticism. Like the critic of theatre or literature, the art critic comments on newly produced art on show to the public in galleries and museums. The art critic offers the public

Words to Remember

interpretation

significance

movements

styles

judgements

influences

appraisal

personal response

critical appraisal of the artwork, while also adding his or her own personal response to the work. This critique may or may not include comparisons with the work of other artists from the same or different periods to back up his judgement about the value of the work on show. Art criticism can be humorous, and it can be very biting and judgmental. Often, it can make or break the reputation of the artist.

For many students, writing about art and design can at first be a bit of a struggle. They have opted for art because they enjoy the practical side of the course. This should not put you off writing or talking about the works of mature or historically significant artists and designers. Art and Design studies are about all those aspects of the subject which help you to develop your knowledge, skills and understanding.

Reading or researching topics in art and design therefore helps you with practical work and increases your vocabulary, makes you more confident about writing and talking and helps you to express your own ideas more clearly.

In Art and Design Studies you deal mainly with mature and recognised artists and designers. Reading and writing about their work will help you to understand the methods and processes that they use. This will help you to develop your own practical work.

Appreciation, understanding and enjoyment of art and design are the long-term benefits of your work in this area. In the short-term it can mean finding out how other artists and designers from the past and present have gone about solving similar problems to those that face you in your art and design course. Studying and writing about the works of artists and designers can be a means of improving your practical work.

In a two-way process some of what you learn through your practical work is useful in Art and Design Studies. For example, if your practical work is about still life or portraiture, you're likely to have found out about how to compose your work or how to get light and dark tones in your work. This is a bit of preparation and knowledge that you can carry over when you look at the works of mature artists who have produced still lifes and portraits.

In conclusion, writing about art and design can be fun and should allow you to combine the practical work with the understanding that comes from studying the works of mature artists and designers.

Writing about Contemporary Visual Art

In the examination you will most likely have the choice of a question on contemporary art. A lot of contemporary art does not fit into the model of analysis that you would use for a more traditional example.

All art was contemporary once. Art is always breaking new ground and this is as true in the twenty-first century as it has been throughout the history of art. Often you can feel completely at a loss when confronting a new idea or image. How do you respond to contemporary works when your first response is 'I don't understand this'?

Mark Wallinger's Sleeper (2004)
video projection (silent), 2 hours 31 mins

The Turner prize is awarded annually for contemporary art. In 2007, the artist Mark Wallinger entered a single work – a video of himself dressed in a furry bear suit wandering, as if in a daze, around a modern art gallery in Berlin.

For ten nights, Wallinger was locked into the art gallery alone. On the final night, he filmed himself in the costume on three cameras pacing the floors, gazing at onlookers outside through glass windows and slumping to the ground.

You should know that many contemporary artists set out deliberately to challenge our accepted knowledge and thinking about art, so a feeling of not knowing or disorientation is quite common. However, it is sometimes when you are most challenged in your reactions to an unfamiliar and unseen contemporary work that you get the deepest insights into what the artist is trying to communicate. Wallinger, like many contemporary artists, challenges us to think about what makes art *art*.

Of all the burning questions about much contemporary art is the basic question 'But is it art at all?' Some contemporary artists use unconventional materials and ways of working that we do not usually associate with artistic production.

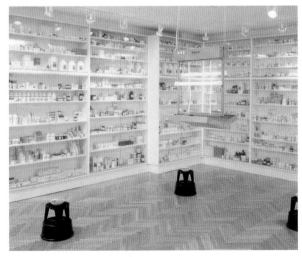

Others try to get you to think about materials and ideas in new ways. They set out to be deliberately provocative in order to challenge your thinking about issues affecting our lives such as identity. They also provoke strong emotions such as protest, love and hate.

Damien Hirst, Pharmacy (2001)

Rachel Whiteread's works are casts of objects that we use or inhabit every day. When she cast the house on Bow Road it was the last remaining Victorian terrace house in an old street in London. Her work is the product of craftsmanship in the way in which the inside of the house has been carefully assembled from concrete casts.

Another problem that we have is deciding whether some contemporary art is 'good'. Sometimes we question the lack of traditional skills in contemporary visual art. Throughout the twentieth century, for example, many artists produced art that was not realistic. In dealing with contemporary art you should try to go beyond the idea that realism is the only appropriate form of depiction and that the skills of the contemporary artist are not always about the craft of using paint and drawing well. Today's artists very often do not even make the art that you see. Some, like David Mach, will use many volunteers to help him build his installations. Others, like Donald Judd, will employ people to make the work for him.

There is no reason why art cannot be made from new materials. In recent times artists have made art from 'found objects' such as bricks, plastic rubbish, crushed cars and even elephant dung! Ever since the artist Marcel Duchamp created a work of art out of a urinal, artists have looked for 'ready-mades' to assemble a composition from materials not normally associated with art.

Much contemporary art is not designed for the limited spaces of galleries or the space above the fireplace in the home of a collector. You will find a lot of it in public spaces. Douglas Gordon and Christine Borland make a lot of their work in this way so that a wide range of people can experience it.

Contemporary means more than simply done in the last 25 years. It refers to art that tends to challenge the existing conventions and traditional methods of making art. Contemporary artists want the viewer to be active. Their work can take the form of a performance; it can be short lived; and it can be disseminated over the Internet and downloaded on to your mp3 player much in the same way as music. In looking at contemporary art you have to be aware of all these possibilities.

It is not possible to categorise all contemporary art into movements and styles. You may come across terms like Post-modern, Neo Romantic or categories like 'Brit Art'. It is unlikely that you will find the kind of similarities here that you would among Impressionist artists such as Monet and Pissarro or Surrealist artists such as Dali and Magritte.

You may not be able to apply all of the questions associated with content, form, process and mood to every example of contemporary art. Instead, it may help you to try to *classify* the piece that you are examining. Here are some classifications.

INSTALLATION ART

If it is in a gallery, an installation will usually take up an entire room. The work will sometimes combine different media and materials and may include sculpture, moving images and sound. You have to imagine yourself in the space that the artist has created, walking around and reacting to the messages that the artist is communicating in the work. Installation is not confined to gallery spaces. Indeed, for many artists it is a way of showing that the experience of art need not simply be in an art gallery.

David Mach, 101 Dalmatians (1988)

SITE-SPECIFIC ART / ENVIRONMENTAL ART

Site-specific or Environmental art is work that is made for a particular location. Artists such as Andy Goldsworthy use the actual materials of the site in the composition. Antony Gormley used the site high above the A1 motorway to place the famous *Angel of the North,* which acts as a greeting to visitors to Gateshead.

NEW TECHNOLOGIES

This describes artists who work with new digital technologies like Bruce Nauman and Bill Viola. Their work is usually done with video and combined with installation.

POLITICAL

Political artists use their work to oppose power and control. They challenge what we consider to be acceptable forms and content of art. Helen Chadwick, Gilbert and George, Damien Hirst, Tracy Emin and Susan Hillier all produce very different contemporary works, but each explores political themes in their compositions.

ART FOR SOCIAL ACTION

These are artists who deal with social issues and who want their work to provoke action in the community.

LAND ART

Land artists such as Richard Long work directly in the landscape, sculpting it into earthworks or producing very large-scale works out of rocks and stones found in the landscape.

1.1

Portraiture

If you are using this section of the book you will probably have been attempting to draw or paint portraits. You will know what you have been doing in practical terms, but can you explain it?

A portrait is the image that results from an interaction between an artist and the sitter. In the case of self-portraits, both are the same. Usually the sitter will want to show a particular image of themselves to the world and the artist will want to show that image in a certain way. A portrait is the result.

Within the period you are studying there has been a huge change in what we understand to be a portrait. From 1750 to today, styles and fashions in art have changed dramatically and, by and large, portraiture has changed with them. You should be aware of these transitions so that you can comment on them in your answers.

In your examination you will have to answer one question on portraiture, with Parts A and B. Part A will involve you studying an illustrated example of a portrait. The work will come from the period you have been studying i.e. 1750 to the present day. It could be in any medium; it may not be a painting, but a collage, sculpture or photograph. The means and materials of its production will be given as well as its size. This information is very important to you when examining the illustration, as it will help you interpret and understand what you are looking at.

Generally, the questions will be about composition, technique and use of visual elements. You may also be asked to comment on the sitter's personality, character or background, as well as the emotional response you have on viewing the portrait. You should therefore always consider these things when looking at artists' work and preparing for your exam. Practise giving your opinion on the works in question and justifying your comments as these are important aspects of your exam responses.

Jean Auguste Dominique Ingres, Portrait of Madame Moitessier (1856)
oil on canvas 120x92 cm

Candidates are asked to discuss the above painting, the composition and pose, the use of visual elements, and to comment on the sitter's probable background.

Ingres portrays the status and personality of Madame Moitessier with the use of pose composition and visual elements. Her status is a very beautiful and well off woman. This is shown by her pose which is very strong and elegant.◄ The use of the floral pattern dress and lots of gold and diamonds also show her wealth.◄ The composition shows that she is not a shy woman, the use of her seating position and the use of her hand near her face shows that she must be very well known to many people and of a very high class.◄ Her personality is very vain, she is beautiful and she knows it.◄ The use of the visual elements such as the mirror shows that she wanted this painting to show every side of her beauty.◄ The use of her hand near her face gives a great visual impact as it makes you look at her face first, like a direction arrow.◄ I think this is a beautiful painting, the artist has used colour very well and the use of the mirror is unusual but works very well.◄

(◄ indicates a point worthy of 1 mark)

The answer in this example is worth about 6 or 7 marks. This person comments on the pose and composition and draws reasonable conclusions. The classical pose suggests self-assurance, while the extravagant dress suggests wealth. The reference to the mirror as an indicator of her personality is also good. There is, however, some confusion as to what the visual elements (the mirror) are and they should have been explored more thoroughly. A complete answer would have commented on pattern, tone, form and media handling. Try to rewrite the response making as many points as you can – try for 10.

Part B questions deal with your knowledge of the working methods and practices of renowned artists from the period 1750 to the present day. You will be asked to compare the work of two prominent artists or movements. In Higher, they should be from different time periods. You will be expected to have a thorough understanding of their work, the influences on them and their influences on others.

The question may ask you to comment on their choice of subjects, styles or working methods. You may be expected to comment on composition, media handling or use of the visual elements. An award of up to 16 marks is generally given to this part of the answer, with a further 4 marks available for the explanation of the importance of the artists in the development of their chosen fields of work.

Discuss examples of portraiture by two artists from different movements or periods. Comment on their choice of subjects, styles and working methods. Explain why you consider your chosen artists to be important.

Impressionism began around 1863 when the Salon des Refuses opened. Many artists' work had been rejected by the official salon for not fitting the required criteria. The first Impressionists were Manet, who was born in 1832 and is sometimes called the 'father of Impressionism', and Renoir. They began to experiment with new techniques and subjects for their work.◄ The invention of photography meant that fine, detailed paintings were no longer needed and the invention of tubes of paint made it easier for artists to paint outside.◄ Also, about this time, Paris was being redesigned to include more areas for leisure activities so artists began to include them in their paintings.◄ Edouard Manet was one of the first Impressionists and I find that the contemporary artist Lucien Freud has been greatly influenced by Manet. Their work is similar though very different and I will show how in my chosen examples.◄

The Bar at the Folies Bergere, by Manet

This painting shows a woman serving at a bar. The use of bright but also dark colours shows that Manet was beginning to introduce characteristics of Impressionism into his work.◄ Manet never considered himself an official member of the movement because he did not want to be known for rebelling against the official system. In Manet's work there are some typical Impressionist ways of painting but also some of the traditional ways of painting.◄ Firstly, the Impressionists were known for painting outdoors but Manet is showing an indoor scene. Another characteristic of Impressionism is heavy, thick brushstrokes with not much detail shown. Manet has used this technique in the background in which only the basic shapes of the people in the crowd can be made out.◄ In the reflection in the mirror Manet has not used a lot of detail, this is different from the barmaid's face that is detailed, painted with fine brushstrokes.◄ Although he has used a lot of dark colours, he has introduced the idea of light on the subject's face and arms. These areas are so bright compared to the rest of the painting that they almost seem to shine.◄ The Impressionists were also keen on capturing snapshots in time, which sometimes make their paintings look slightly awkward. This is shown in Manet's work through the barmaid's pose as it must have been awkward for the woman to stand in that way for the long time it took to be painted.◄

Lucien Freud, *Red haired man on a chair*

Freud has been greatly influenced by Impressionism, particularly by Manet, because he uses similar techniques such as including far more detail in the subject of the painting than in the background. However, in Manet's painting there is still some detail in the background whereas in Freud's painting, the background is just a large area of colour separated by a white band behind the subject.◄ Another Impressionist, Degas, used this technique in order to keep the attention on the subject not the background. Manet's choice of subject is quite formal whereas Freud's is squatting on a chair. Freud's subject also seems a lot more awkward than Manet's and looks very uncomfortable.◄ Freud seems to have taken this awkwardness and made it very obvious to anyone looking at the painting. Freud, like Manet, also uses lighter colour on the subject's face and hands that are painted using finer brushstrokes.◄ However, Freud, who uses a lighter palette, does not use Manet's contrasts between very light and very dark colours. This suggests that other Impressionists who used lighter, brighter colours have influenced Freud.◄

Manet's and Freud's styles of painting are very different because Freud has a much more relaxed way of painting. Their subjects are also different because Manet chose to paint much more formal subjects.◄ They use similar working methods except that Freud uses less detail over-all and lighter brushstrokes. I consider both of these artists very important as they have been an influence on many other artists in the past and will continue to influence artists in the future.◄

(◄ indicates a point worthy of 1 mark)

The essay example above is quite good and would score about 15 or 16 marks at Higher. This person has chosen examples from artists of differing periods that can allow for contrasts in style or working methods to be shown. A different example of Manet's work may have been chosen that was more appropriate to a portraiture question. Although we know the name of the barmaid, the painting, with it's prominent still life objects in the foreground and reflected crowds in the background, may be seen as more of a portrait of the place than of the individual. This was not brought out in the answer. Throughout there are statements made but not explored in detail. The final paragraph does not really say why the artists are important, just that they are. There was a lack of depth in the response that prevented it from achieving a higher mark. Try rewriting the example above, adding more information to complete the answer.

When practising the activities outlined, you should be mindful of the time available to you in the exam. Part A questions at Higher should take around 15 minutes, whereas Part B answers may require about 30 minutes. Use a timer when you practise in order to get used to the time constraints.

Francis Bacon, Self-portrait (1971)
oil on canvas 35.5x30.5 cm

So, What is a Portrait?

This would seem a simple question to answer, but in forming an answer other questions arise. Is it a painting, or, more commonly today, a photograph, or maybe a piece of film?   Yes, it may be any of these, but it could also be a piece of sculpture, a bust (a portrait of a head and shoulders, usually sculpture), full figure or low relief. Throughout history there has been a practice of coins carrying the portrait of the current ruler or monarch. One definition may be that a portrait is a likeness of an individual. (But not all portraits are likenesses.)

There are portraits that aim to flatter the sitter in some way, for instance portraits of important politicians or monarchs are often full length, painted from a low angle in an attempt to make the subject appear superior or more important than the viewer. Many of these portraits of important people are large in scale and are intended to be seen in grand public rooms or open spaces.

Now try this...

Find three portraits of famous people, living or dead. They may be paintings, drawings or photographs (books and the Internet are probably your best source of reference).

- Are they formal, posed compositions?

- From what angle do we see the sitter?

- Was the sitter aware the portrait was being made?

- How have the visual elements (line, tone, colour, shape, form, texture etc.) been used?

- Does the way the visual elements have been used help set a particular mood or atmosphere in the portraits?

- Compare them, considering the way the artist/photographer has composed the portrait.

- Which one is most successful?

- Justify your opinion.

During certain periods in the past, artists and connoisseurs had a very strict idea of what beauty was. In those times portraits were produced according to especially strict rules, often based on ideas from the past. The French Neoclassical artists Ingres and David looked at the art of ancient Greece and Rome for inspiration. On other occasions artists looked to the sculptures from different cultures as a source of inspiration.

Picasso's portrait of Gertrude Stein was done just after he had been studying African and Roman sculpture, and just before he began to develop Cubism. Although Stein sat for the portrait on over ninety occasions, Picasso eventually painted the head from memory without Stein being present. His final image was not an observed study of his subject, rather a remembered idea of her. The influence of the sculpture he had been studying can be seen in the face. When a visitor who had seen the portrait said it did not look like Stein, Picasso replied, "It will".

*Picasso, Portrait of Gertrude Stein (1906)
oil on canvas 100x81.3 cm*

Now try this...

a) Discuss the methods used by Picasso to show the sitter's character. Comment on composition of the painting and the artist's use of tone and handling of paint. What is your reaction to the portrait?

b) Discuss the work of two artists from different periods whose portraiture you have admired. Explain why you consider them to be important artists in this field.

In some paintings artists have used live models when representing characters in a composition. On these occasions the paintings will have been true likenesses of individuals, but the paintings are not portraits. This is most usually the case when the subject of the painting is not really the people in it, but the surroundings or event being shown.

Toulouse-Lautrec's figure paintings were completed using sketches and drawings he had made from observation of friends and acquaintances. Here, the two dancers were professional performers in the dance halls and theatres of Paris and are shown during their act. Other figures in the painting were acquaintances of

*Henri Toulouse-Lautrec, The Dance at the
Moulin Rouge (1889-90)
oil on canvas 115.5x150 cm*

Toulouse-Lautrec and characters seen around Montmartre, the area in which he lived. The painting, although showing actual likenesses, is not a portrait.

A portrait can be described as a work of art about a person or group of people. Another definition of a portrait may be a work where the artist tries to show the character of an individual. But even this definition may not cover all aspects of portraiture.

Throughout history people have felt the need to record the likenesses of both the living and the dead. From Ancient Egypt we have likenesses of Pharaohs and other members of the Royal family dating from as far back as 3000 BC. The Greeks and the Romans also left us with portrait heads and statues of emperors and other important individuals. Paintings on the walls of Pompeii from the first century AD record likenesses of individuals from that period.

In the middle ages wealthy patrons who gifted religious paintings to the church sometimes asked the artist to include portraits of them in the religious painting. These paintings became known as 'donor portraits'. Often in these pictures the donor would be shown in profile, in contrast with the idealised images of the saints or other holy persons who were the principal subject of the picture and were usually seen looking out of the picture towards the viewer. Showing the donor in profile may just be a convention, or it may have been because it is less complicated in some ways to paint a profile than a frontal view. Profiles can be created by drawing round a shadow of the sitter's profile, thus achieving an accurate likeness.

Achieving a likeness in a portrait is always a challenge for the artist. Unlike the camera, which simply records the appearance of the subject, artists and photographers interpret the character and give clues to the sitter's personality in a number of ways. If we think of a well-known politician or personality, we know

ABOVE: J D Fergusson, In the Patio: Margaret Morris Fergusson (1925) oil on canvas 71x61 cm

LEFT: John Byrne, Billy Connolly (2002) oil on canvas 54x39 cm

them from numerous photographs taken of them. But we are also able to recognise them when they are shown as caricatures, either in sketch or puppet form. The artist, in these instances, will tend to emphasise or distort some prominent feature of the sitter in order to achieve recognition. With even a small amount of visual information we can make the correct interpretation. Some artists manage to elevate caricatures to a fine art form, their portrayal of the subject being influenced by either fondness or disapproval.

A skilled portraitist is also capable of this. Gainsborough or Whistler, for instance, could simplify a face with a few loose brushstrokes but maintain a likeness when doing so. Nearer our time, some of the portraits by J D Fergusson are very simple in their portrayal of the face.

Now try this...

a) Discuss the way in which Fergusson portrays the character of his wife. Comment on the use of composition, colour and media handling. What is the most important visual element used in the painting?

b) Compare the work of two artists from different periods or movements who use contrasting approaches to portraiture. Comment on their subjects, working methods and style.

In his portrayal of Mao Tse-Tung, Andy Warhol took the portrait from the cover of a book of Mao Tse-Tung's quotations and then printed it in various sizes on canvas. The prints were coloured in a variety of ways, not using natural colour. Warhol did not carefully register the different colours, leaving us with an image that, in its final presentation, reminds us that it is a print.

Andy Warhol, Mao Tse-Tung (1972)
screenprint and paint on canvas 91.6x91.4 cm

Although catching a likeness is sometimes achieved through simplification and mild distortion of the sitter's features, it can still exist even after severe manipulation and distortion. Francis Bacon, for example, often widely distorted the features of the people he painted, but we only have to look at photographs taken of his subjects to see how he managed to maintain a resemblance throughout. Indeed some people maintain that Bacon's portraits strip away the superficial and get to the essence of the sitter's personality.

When we examine portraits we begin to recognise a range of poses used time and again by artists. The most common would be the 'frontal' or 'three-quarter' pose where the sitter looks directly at the viewer. The look can either be engaging, almost intimate or, as is often the case in portraits of monarchs or aristocracy, distant. The sitter may be standing or seated full figure or be shown close-up. The artist will often pose the sitter in a comfortable pose in order not to tire them too much while the work is being done.

The facial expression shown may be a smile, a grimace or neutral. Sometimes the face is shown in slight shadow which tells us little about the sitter. The direction in which the subject is looking will frequently tell us most. Eyes can look straight at us or glance from the side in an almost shifty manner. They may be looking away, perhaps at something in the distance or as if in a dream.

A large number of portraits show the sitter against a plain or self-coloured background. We presume in these cases that the artist has not wished to distract us from the facial likeness. At other times we see the sitter surrounded with their possessions, thus adding to our knowledge of the person being portrayed. Sometimes a decorative or patterned background is used.

Now try this...

Find three portraits in which the artist has used a highly patterned background.

Does the background make it more or less easy to focus on the sitter's face?

Is colour an important element? Does it unify the painting or is it used to contrast sitter and background?

How is tone used in the picture? Does it unite the elements of composition or separate them?

What does the use of a patterned background suggest to us about the sitter?

Renoir, The Luncheon of the Boating Party (1881)
oil on canvas 129x172 cm

Keep in mind that not all portraits are of single individuals. Early group portraits often showed kings and their courts or groups of individuals linked by interest or profession. The Impressionists showed ordinary people enjoying their leisure time.

Portraits of married couples were sometimes painted to celebrate the marriage. Paintings like this one by Gainsborough showed not only the people concerned but also their possessions. Indeed the possessions were, on occasion, almost as important as the individuals shown. Whatever the reason for the double portrait, they almost all suggest some sort of relationship between the sitters.

Thomas Gainsborough, Mr and Mrs Andrews
(1750) oil on canvas 69x119 cm

The placing of the individual within the picture reflected their status. Until the nineteenth century it was common practice to place the husband on the left side of the painting slightly above the wife i.e. in a superior position. In the twentieth century this ceased to be the case; indeed, the artist David Hockney reversed the positions of the sexes in his painting Mr. and Mrs. Clark and Percy.

David Hockney, Mr. and Mrs. Clark and Percy
(1970) acrylic on canvas 304x213 cm

*Edgar Degas, Monsieur and Madame Manet
(1879) oil on canvas 65x71 cm*

As photographic portraits became more common, painters began to reassess the purpose of the painted portrait. After all, the camera could record a likeness in one visit to the photographers studio as opposed to many sittings needed for a painting. There was also the difference in cost. As its popularity became widespread, the costs of photography decreased until even the most humble could own portraits of their nearest and dearest. However, where the early monochrome photograph recorded realistic images, the artist could respond in paint in a subjective manner. The use of brushstrokes, texture and colour produced an animated surface contrasting with that of the early photograph.

Artists such as Degas did, however, use photography as a means of exploring composition and recording models in particular poses. Generally, however, the Impressionists reacted to photography by becoming increasingly involved in the depiction of light and colour.

Degas' portrait of Manet and his wife would have been seen as an unconventional image when it was painted. The composition is unusual in its informality. Manet is lounging at rest and his wife's face is cut off by the screen on the right of the picture. When we compare it with photographic studies and some of the compositions seen in Japanese prints – which were popular around that time – we can see a link.

One way artists responded to the development of photography was to treat the portrait as a formal composition in its own right rather than just a representational work. Austrian artist Gustav Klimt was a master of this. Many of his portraits of women, while maintaining a true likeness of the sitter, were also quite abstract, rich in decoration and at times extravagant exhibitions of carefully designed pattern. Others, such as Matisse and Picasso, went even further at times producing works that were difficult to recognise as people, let alone likenesses of particular individuals.

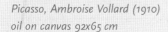

Picasso, Ambroise Vollard (1910)
oil on canvas 92x65 cm

Picasso, Head of a Woman (Fernande) (1909)
bronze 40.6x26x25.4 cm

Both of the portraits by Picasso shown above were done around the same time when he was working in a Cubist style.

Compare the artist's methods in producing each of the works. Which technique do you think is most suited to describing the sitter?

Which portrait shows us most about the sitter's interests or personality?

Which one do you consider to be most successful as a portrait? Justify your answer.

The Cubist's aim was not to produce a likeness to the subject, but rather a response to it. The artist portrayed not the public image of the sitter, but the artist's idea of him. Throughout his life Picasso continued to use formal distortion in his portraits while maintaining the essence of his sitter's appearance.

One situation where the portrait was to become very important was in photographic stills of Hollywood film stars. The early studios wanted their famous stars to be shown in their best light, often in situations suggesting their character in their latest film. The studio employed skilful photographers and the resulting portraits were distributed throughout the world.

Twentieth century artists working in different movements often painted portraits in the style of the movement, rather than trying for a realistic likeness of the sitter. They did, however, usually strive to portray some aspect of the sitter's personality through the images they produced.

Henri Matisse, Green Stripe (1905)
oil and tempera on canvas 40x30 cm

Otto Dix, Portrait of the Journalist Sylvia von Harden (1926)
oil and tempera on canvas 121x89 cm

Look carefully at the two paintings above and compare them. Consider the artists' use of colour, composition and media handling.

What does each painting say about the personality of the sitter?

Which painting do you consider to be the most successful as a portrait? Justify your opinions.

The way in which the artist is regarded by society has allowed these changes to take place. Artists are no longer reliant on patrons who commission work for their private collections – the powerful people who expected to be portrayed in a certain way. Rather, artists tend to be represented by dealers and their work sold through galleries where the display is public rather than private. This allows more freedom for the artist to work in a manner personal to him. The artist now regularly chooses the subject rather than it being chosen by a sitter. The consequence of this is that much of a modern portrait artist's work may be of friends and family rather than of commissioning patrons. These works are frequently quite intimate, both in feeling and in scale. An artist who portrays friends and acquaintances almost exclusively, but also works on a grand scale, is the American artist Chuck Close.

Chuck Close, John (1972)
acrylic on canvas 250x225 cm

Close's work is based on a grid, where individual elements of the whole are painted separate from the others. By using this process, Close is able to work on a piece over an extended period (often months at a time) with interruptions but without compromising the final product. This allows him to come and go while working on various projects. From a distance Close's paintings look like photographs, but in actuality each individual grid-piece is painted by hand.

One other form of portraiture not requiring commissioning is the self-portrait. Throughout history artists have produced images of themselves. For one thing, it is convenient as a model is not required. The self-portrait is sometimes used by artists to practice their art; perhaps investigating aspects of lighting or composition. Self-portraits also act as an advertisement for the artist's skill, in that artists often show themselves as thoughtful or successful people, or record aspects of their lives.

In this way, Vincent van Gogh follows a long-standing tradition where artists record changes to their appearance throughout their lives. Whether it is a self-portrait, or a portrait of a sitter, we can be sure that the fascination with examining human existence will see portraiture continue as a popular artistic activity long into the future.

Renoir,
The Boat Party

Gainsborough,
Mr and Mrs Andrews

Closely examine the two group portraits above.

What is the most important visual element in each (line, tone, colour, shape, form etc.)?

Compare and contrast the artists' use of media and composition. What does each painting tell us about the sitters?

Which one do you prefer? Say why.

We can sometimes also follow the state of the artist's moods and emotions. In the case of van Gogh we see a series of paintings where he looks clearly and in a detached way at himself, honestly recording what he sees.

These self-portraits were painted not long before van Gogh died.

Do you think they suggest anything about his feelings when he painted them?

Does his paint technique contribute to the atmosphere of the works? If so, how?

Which painting do you think is most successful? Justify your answer.

Self-portrait with bandaged ear (1889)
oil on canvas 60.5x50 cm

Self-portrait with felt hat (1888)
oil on canvas 44x37.5 cm

Exam Preparation

In preparing for your exam you should look in detail at the work of at least **two** different artists or art movements. You should know their background thoroughly, and who influenced them. Find out if they have been an influence on artists who followed, and if they were influential in the development of portraiture.

Do not limit your research to a couple of examples from each artist or movement. The better informed you are, the more completely you will be able to answer the question paper. Remember that past papers are just a guide to the type of questions that have been asked in previous years. The examiners are always refining the style of question you may be asked. If you have a thorough knowledge of your subject you will be able to respond to changes in questioning.

When looking at a portrait we should attempt to understand how the artist approached the work and what his or her main concerns were. Ask yourself questions like the ones that follow to make sure you are fully prepared.

Who made it? Do you know the name of the artist or anything about them? Having previous knowledge about the artist often helps our appreciation of a piece of artwork.

When was it made? Knowing when the work was made can help our understanding of why it was created. The conditions of the time can have an effect on how the artist approached the task. Technological changes have, throughout history, had an effect on how artists approach their work.

What is the subject matter? Is the work a realistic portrayal of the sitter? Is the response purely accurate or is there an emotional element to it? Try to identify if the artist is concerned with depicting a particular aspect of the sitter's personality. If the work is a group portrait, look closely to see if a relationship between any of the sitters is suggested. Determine if the effects of light have been intensified or distorted to heighten an emotion, and if the background of the portrait is important in telling us something about the sitter.

What is the format of the work? What size is it? Decide if it has been made to be viewed in a specific environment. Discover what the work is made from and how the medium has been used. Establish if a particular technique or style of working has been used, and whether it has contributed to the overall effect of the work.

By answering these questions, as well as those you come up with yourself, you will be preparing yourself to give thorough responses on your exam papers.

1.2

Figure Composition

If you are using this section you will probably be involved in producing practical work under the heading of Figure Composition. Most likely you will have been working with drawings and photographs of models, posed in positions appropriate to the theme you are following. It is also likely that you will have an awareness of the challenges working in this area presents to the artist.

Some of these concerns deal with capturing particular poses or facial expressions in your models. Others involve the problem of finding visual resources to use in the background of your work to help explain your theme. This, again, could take the form of drawings or photographs.

Perhaps you will be constructing a wholly imaginative background in which to place the figures. Some of the challenges you will be faced with involve determining perspective, describing distance and space, and trying to set a mood or feeling in your work. Through the use of particular tonal or colour ranges, you have an opportunity to suggest a variety of moods. Do you want a feeling of drama and tension or calm and stillness?

Like portraiture, you will need to decide the format you will work in. What materials will allow you to best express your ideas? Will you be painting with watercolour or using thick impasto? If using dry media such as crayons or chalks, will you allow the marks of the drawing medium to show or will you blend your colours and tones?

Perhaps your work will be 3-D. Will you be happy with one medium or will you use mixed media, perhaps printing or collage? How will the proportions of scale of your work contribute to its overall effectiveness? Will it be small and intimate, encouraging the viewer to get close and examine the detail carefully, or will it be big and bold, best taken in from a distance?

If you have been considering these sorts of questions in relation to your own work you will have been doing the same thing as the famous artists whose work you will be studying as part of your Art Studies unit. When you look at their work ask yourself these same questions in relation to it. This will help you gain a better understanding of the artists' intentions, and in turn inspire and help you with your own work.

Part A questions will involve you studying an illustrated example of a figure composition. The work will come from the period you have been studying i.e. 1750 to the present day. It could be in any medium; it may not be a painting, but a

these and other props to give an 'element of mysticism'.◀ In her Bathers painting none of the figures are actually in the water because Watt herself has an intense fear of water. Watt's figures are very statuesque and contrived.

(◀ indicates a point worthy of 1 mark)

This essay shows quite a good understanding of the work of both artists, and is worth about 15 marks. The writer has described examples of both artists' work, though comparisons are implied rather than being specific.

The bulk of the essay discusses Manet's work and it feels that the writer had run out of time when describing Watt's approach. The references to influences on both artists are good and the choice of examples backs up the points being made. The reasons they are regarded to be successful is implied rather than stated. The candidates reasons for thinking both artists to be important are clear in the case of Manet, but less so in relation to Watt.

Could you structure an essay that answered the question with more clarity and would gain full marks?

Why Work with Figure Composition?

Artists use figures in their work for a number of reasons. One of the most basic is our fascination with our own species and our interest in it. We are keen to examine experiences and emotions generally common to most of us: joy, happiness, suffering, fear etc. These can be shown in art terms through a number of subjects or themes.

Going back into our past, religion has provided a rich source of subject matter for the artist interested in mankind. Religious art has focused on such subjects as the creation of Man, good and evil, and life after death. The artist was generally an illustrator of Biblical stories, employed by wealthy patrons of the church to produce works that promote a Christian view and glorify God.

It is generally accepted that the Renaissance was born in fourteenth-century Florence. There, the wealthy Medici family commissioned artists such as Leonardo da Vinci, Botticelli, Michelangelo and Raphael. They produced work of outstanding quality, much of it in a religious theme. By the fifteenth and sixteenth centuries in Italy, such works reach an outstanding quality. Many of the acknowledged masterpieces of Western art were produced at this time. As artists, we are indebted to the Renaissance for our understanding of anatomy and perspective.

The ideas of the Renaissance travelled throughout Europe during the following centuries, evolving over time. In the fifteenth-century in the Netherlands, Jan van Eyck perfected the use of oil paint and canvas, creating remarkable effects with the medium. (Much of the Italian painting was done directly onto the walls of buildings using egg tempera.) Unlike the religious themes of the Italian artists, some artists in the Netherlands began painting portrayals of everyday life and landscapes. Over time, ideas on art flowed between the two regions in both directions.

As well as religion, the illustration of mythology, the representation and recording of historical events and scenes from everyday life have provided figurative artists with a rich source of inspiration.

ABOVE: Paolo Veronese, The Marriage at Cana (1562-63) oil on canvas 6.7x9.9 metres

BELOW: David, Oath of the Horatti (1734) oil on canvas 329x424 cm

Remember, the period you are studying begins after the Renaissance, but it is an advantage to have some knowledge of what preceded it. These artists are not within the time frame of your exam. They are included to broaden your understanding of the history of figure composition.

At the beginning of the study period we have Neoclassicism and Romanticism. The most prominent Neoclassical artists were David and Ingres, while Delacroix and Gericault represent Romanticism. They all specialised in figure composition.

The Neoclassical artists rejected the flamboyance of Baroque art that had gone before it. Instead, they adopted themes from ancient Greece and Rome to express in their paintings ideas on loyalty, patriotism and sacrifice. This is readily seen in their work. In David's painting *Oath of the Horatti,* the principal figures are painted in stronger colours than the muted tones of the background. They are shown in clear focus, smoothly painted with no brushstrokes evident. This helps to emphasise the statue-like poses the figures adopt and promotes a mood of control and rationality even in a dramatic situation.

Delacroix, Liberty Leading the People (1830)
oil on canvas 260 x 325 cm

Delacroix, from the Romantic Movement, took his inspiration from a different source. As well as taking his themes from legend and poetry, his artistic influences were Michelangelo and Rubens. In his painting, the emphasis is on colour and movement, rather than form and line as had been the main focus of the Neoclassicists. His use of glazed layers of colourful, broken hatching to show shadow was at odds with the smooth application of paint used by the Neoclassical painters, and was to be an influence on the Impressionists. His most famous Romantic painting is *Liberty Leading the People*. In it he includes a self-portrait, showing himself to the left of the central figure, wearing a top hat.

Following on from his politically-based works, Delacroix became intrigued with northern African culture. Fascination with the exotic was another feature of the Romantic Movement.

During the second half of the nineteenth century, from about 1860–1880, there evolved a style of painting that we call Realism. It rejected the fantasy of the Romantic Movement and replaced it with an art based on observation of the ordinary world, taking commonplace events and situations as its inspiration. Courbet, Daumier and Millet were French Realists. In Britain, the Pre-Raphaelites were a band of artists who drew directly from nature. The subject matter of their later work was based on medieval mythology, but they continued to draw from nature in preparing and researching their paintings.

Now try this...

Find examples by two artists whose work shows how ordinary people live their lives.

What art media have they used e.g. painting, drawing, photography etc.?

How has their technique helped show their subject in a convincing manner?

LEFT: Manet, Music in the Tuileries Gardens (1862) oil on canvas 76x118 cm

BELOW: Degas, Women Ironing (1884) oil on canvas 76x81 cm

Figure composition was an important theme for a number of the Impressionists. Manet's *Dejeuner sur l'herbe* (1863) shocked French society of the time, while his busy composition *Music in the Tuileries Gardens* (above) gives us a record of how French middle classes relaxed. Among the crowd are: Manet and his brother Eugene, the poets Baudelaire and Théophile Gautier, the composer Offenbach and fellow painter Henri Fantin-Latour.

Renoir also shows us Parisians relaxing in paintings such as *The Luncheon on the Boating Party* (1881) and *Ball at the Moulin de la Galette* (1876), while Degas gives us a picture of people at work in the theatre in such pieces as *In the Orchestra Pit* (1869) or *Cabaret* (1875). Degas also shows us mundane workplaces such as the women working in hat shops or in a laundry. His subject matter was predominantly urban, recording either the lives of the expanding middle classes of Paris, or the people who provided services for them.

Other Impressionists such as Mary Cassatt or Berthe Morisot, who were to some extent restricted by themes that were judged suitable for a woman, show us scenes of family life.

Now try this...

With a partner, gather a selection of three or more images in which artists have shown people at work. Make your selection from the period 1850 to today.

Share your findings with your partner, stressing the artists' importance in showing people at work.

Neo-Impressionists, such as Seurat and Signac, continued to use the domestic or leisure activities of the urban population as a rich source of subject matter, but their style of painting was a much more controlled and scientific approach than the spontaneous effects achieved by the Impressionists. The work that resulted, although more rigid and stylised in appearance, does, however, give us a further glimpse into city life of the time.

Cézanne, van Gogh and Gauguin, the Post-Impressionists, each painted significant figure compositions. Cézanne developed his theories on the representation of form and space in such paintings as his *Bathers* series. Here he took a classical theme and adjusted composition, proportion and modelling in his search for a means of representation that went beyond naturalism. He was attempting to describe his subject matter as pure form and to develop a vocabulary and language for artists. His ideas were to be expanded and developed by Picasso and Braque into Cubism.

Vincent van Gogh, The Potato Eaters (1885) oil on canvas 82x114 cm

Van Gogh, who was influenced by Millet in the early stages of his career, painted a number of works depicting peasant life of the time. Paintings such as *The Potato Eaters* are full of energy and capture the simple dignity of his subjects. Although his palette was to become much brighter after his move to the south of France, his forceful brushwork became a signature of his later paintings and was to influence Expressionist artists such as Munch, Nolde and Kirchner.

Gauguin, who for a time worked alongside van Gogh, is renowned for his use of flat colour and shape in his paintings. His subject matter was more mystical, at times dealing with religious or philosophical themes. One of his main influences was African and Eurasian art. He felt that this so-called 'primitive' art was more powerful and successful in portraying raw emotion than current European art. So strong was his desire to experience this first hand that he left his family and went to live in Tahiti where he was to stay for most of the remainder of his life. From then on he produced a remarkable number of paintings, prints and sculptures reflecting the society he found there. Gauguin tried to portray emotion through his use of colour and, in doing so, simplified his drawing and played down the importance of form. He was to be a major influence on the Fauve painters and Expressionists.

The Fauves were a group of painters including Derain, Dufy, Maurice de Vlaminck and Matisse. They got their name from the art critic Louis Vauxcelles, who used the term *Fauves*, the French for 'wild beasts', when describing a collection of their work. Although it was a term of derision, it stuck even when the public accepted their work.

Now try this...

Compare the work of two artists who have used people in conflict as a source of inspiration.

What mood or atmosphere were they trying to show in their work? What techniques did they use to achieve their aims?

How successful have they been? Give examples of their work that illustrates your opinions.

A love of bright expressive colour was what bound the group. They only exhibited three times together between 1905 and 1907, but their interest in colour was to remain important to most of them throughout their working lives. For Matisse, colour and decorative pattern together were to be the most significant elements of his work, allowing him to portray a great joy for life in his paintings.

Paul Gauguin, Mahana noatua (Day of God)
(1894)
oil on canvas 68.3 x 91.5 cm

Matisse, La Musique (1939)
oil on canvas 115x115 cm

Now try this...

a) Discuss the methods used by Matisse to produce this figure composition. Comment on his use of colour, shape and media handling. Explain your thoughts about the painting.

b) Discuss the work of two artists from different periods or movements who have been inspired to show scenes of family life. Give examples of their work that show their response to this theme.

One of the most influential art movements of the twentieth century was Cubism. It was at its height between 1907 and 1914, having been begun by Picasso and Braque. The main influences on Cubism were Cézanne, the Fauves and African sculpture. The Cubists were not interested in representing perspective or form by conventional means. Instead, in their paintings and drawings, they emphasised the two-dimensional surface of the work, showing several views of the subject at the same time. The movement had two main stages. Analytical Cubism predominated from 1908–1912, and is recognised by its use of geometric shapes and planes, as well as subdued almost monochromatic colour. Synthetic Cubism followed and was more decorative, using elements of collage and generally brighter colours. Picasso's painting *Les Demoiselles d' Avignon*, which was heavily influenced by African masks, is generally regarded as being the first Cubist painting. Other artists who worked in a Cubist style included Leger, Gris and Delaunay.

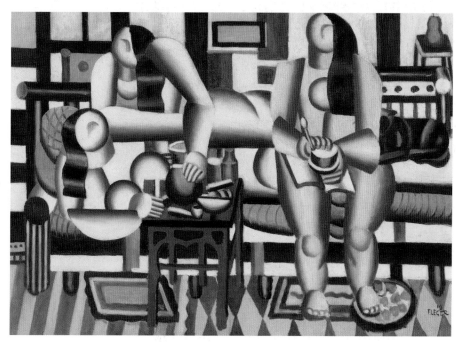

Fernand Leger, Le Petit Dejeuner (1919) oil on canvas 64x92 cm

The Expressionists, who took their influence from van Gogh and the Fauves, were a group of mostly Northern European artists who saw the expression of emotion as being the most important aspect of their art. They valued the expression of their feelings more than the observation of reality. In the early part of the twentieth century in Germany, their art reflected the tensions of city life, often taking a pessimistic view of mankind. Artists such as Dix and Grosz were to use their art for severe political criticism of the emerging Fascist movement and what they saw as the degenerate nature of German society. Among the most prominent Expressionist artists were Beckman, Dix, Kirchner and Nolde, while in France George Rouault produced many expressive works.

Discuss the subject and composition of the Kirchner painting above.

Comment on the artist's use of colour and media handling.

Explain your personal response to this work.

Figure composition remained a popular form of art throughout the twentieth century; it continues to allow us to examine how we behave. British painters such as Stanley Spencer used it to record scenes of shipbuilding on the Clyde during the Second World War, while William Roberts and Willie Rodger use it to examine our social interaction, sometimes with a humorous slant.

ABOVE: *Ernst Ludwig Kirchner, Street Dresden (1908)*
oil on canvas 150x200 cm

LEFT: *William Roberts, The Rhine Boat (1928)*
oil on canvas 50x40 cm

Willie Rodger, Afternoon Bridge (1991)
linocut 15x16 inches

Now try this...

1 What are the main differences in the way Roberts and Rogers have responded to the theme of people at leisure? Consider their use of composition and media.

2 How have they represented the theme of leisure?

3 Discuss the work of two artists from different periods or movements who have taken their inspiration from people at leisure to produce figure composition. Give examples; comment on their working methods and styles. State why they are important artists.

Artists today continue to be interested in recording mankind's interaction with each other in all situations: leisure, work and war. Nearly every kind of human interaction is a source of inspiration to an artist somewhere.

Exam Preparation

In preparing for your exam you should look in detail at the work of at least **two** different artists or art movements. You should know their background thoroughly, including the people who influenced them. Find out, also, if they have been an influence on people who followed, and whether they were influential in the development of figure composition.

Do not limit your research to a couple of examples from each artist or movement. The better informed you are the more completely you will be able to answer the question paper. Remember that past papers are just a guide to the type of questions that have been asked in previous years. The examiners are always refining the style of question you may be asked. If you have a thorough knowledge of your subject you will be able to respond to changes in questioning.

When looking at work based on figure composition you should attempt to understand how the artist approached the work and what his main concerns were. Ask yourself questions like the ones that follow to make sure you are fully prepared.

Who made it? Do you know the name of the artist or anything about them? Previous knowledge often helps our appreciation of a piece of artwork.

When was it made? Knowing when the work was made can help our understanding of why it was created. The conditions of the time can have an effect on how the artist approached the task. Technological changes have, throughout history, had an affect on how artists approached their work.

What is the subject matter? Is the work a realistic depiction of people? Is the response purely accurate or is there an emotional element to it? Determine if the artist is concerned with depicting an aspect of man's character. Is the artist showing us the interaction between people? Determine if the effects of light have been intensified or distorted to heighten an emotion. Is the season or time of day important?

What is the format of the work? What size is it? Decide if it has been made to be viewed in a specific environment. Discover what the work is made from and how the medium has been used. Establish if a particular technique or style of working has been used, and whether it has contributed to the overall effect of the work.

By answering these questions, as well as those you come up with yourself, you will be preparing yourself to give thorough responses on your exam papers.

1.3

Still Life

Looking at Paintings

As part of your course you will be looking at the working methods of artists who painted still life. You will be examining their paintings closely and relating what they did to your own work. Naturally, you will find some artists' work more interesting than others. In order to inform yourself fully and benefit as much as you can in your own work you should therefore look at as wide a range of paintings as is possible. The ideal way to do this is to visit art galleries and see paintings first hand. That allows you to fully understand the artist's methods of working. You can stand in front of a painting and ask yourself questions such as 'How did the artist begin this painting? What part did he do first? What was the last piece of the painting the artist worked on? What part did they do before that?' Looking and questioning in that way will help you better understand how paintings come about.

Some artists are concerned with drawing, some with accuracy, and others with mood or the surface quality of paint. A close-up examination of a painting will help you appreciate the artist's main concern. By looking at many paintings you will find some whose approach is similar to your own and be able to learn from them.

We can be pleasantly surprised, or sometimes even disappointed, when we see an original painting that we know well from books. The image may be much bigger than we had realised and, when seen first hand, be even more powerful than when reproduced on the page. Sometimes a painting that we think is painted in a very realistic 'finished' manner may seem coarser and more broadly worked when viewed in reality.

For many of us, however, regular visits to art galleries are not possible. We have to rely on using books or the Internet as our source of visual information. Both are very good when used correctly but what neither can really do is give us the understanding of the scale of a work or the emotional feeling of being confronted with it first hand. We should therefore try to see the works on as large a scale as possible in order to be able to appreciate their qualities as accurately as we can.

It is good practice to have a broad knowledge of the history of still life, even the times outwith the period you will be primarily concerned with: 1750 to the present day. You will be better able to appreciate the importance of what was happening during the period you are studying if you know a little about what came before it.

Why do Artists Paint Still Life Paintings?

Although still widely practised, still life does not have the potential of some other forms of painting. Its subject matter can have something to say, apart from being a description of a group of objects, but it cannot record events in the way history painting (figure composition) can. Portraiture allows us to comment on human personality and character, and landscape can examine our relationship with the world around us – still lifes are unable to do either of these.

Still life as we are familiar with it really developed in the Netherlands in the seventeenth century. In southern Europe religious themes remained popular, but after the Reformation, still life painting became popular and developed in various forms.

Holland at that time was a prosperous trading nation and still life painting, which is generally of a smaller scale than landscape or figurative painting, allowed the wealthy to exhibit accounts of their success within their homes. The paintings often showed expensive or exotic objects that only the very wealthy could afford, sometimes shown in very rich settings. Even if the purchaser of the painting could not afford the silver ware of fine china shown, the fact that he had a painting of them showed him to be a person of taste.

These paintings were very skilfully done, requiring exceptional ability on the part of the artist. Still life painters of the time could accurately portray the textures of fine fabrics such as velvet, satin and oriental carpets, the surface sheen of delicate glass and rare metals, the patina on musical and scientific instruments and the colours of fresh fish and game.

As well as representing contemporary luxury items, some Dutch still life artists produced paintings of subject matter called 'Vanitas'. These paintings commonly included symbolic items such as: skulls – representing man's mortality; jugs – signifying emptiness; watches or clocks – a reminder that time passes and life has a limited span; an extinguished lamp – indicating death; and other objects whose symbolism was understood.

Likewise, floral paintings have different meanings depending on the flowers portrayed. Lilies for example are associated with purity, irises represent suffering and the rose symbolises love. The educated buyers of such art were aware of this underlying symbolism and still life paintings could therefore form the basis for intellectual discussion. Still life was at its most popular when the art buyers were more interested in paintings that showed things looked at closely, rather than when they were interpretations of stories or work based on imagination.

It was in France that modern still life really came to the fore in the late 1800s. Artists such as Manet and the Impressionists, and later the Post-Impressionists, began to treat still life subjects with the same seriousness as that given to the established forms of academic painting.

The French Academy of Painting did not previously share this view. History painting was believed to be at the pinnacle of artistic achievement while still life was regarded as the lowliest. The artist Chardin was the first to seriously challenge this idea. His carefully constructed compositions, usually of simple domestic objects, won over the academicians. He became the first still life artist to be elected to the French Academy of Art.

Pieter Claesz, Still Life with the Spinario (1628)
oil on canvas 70x80 cm

Most still life artists, however, also practised other forms of painting. Chardin, for instance, also painted domestic scenes, while Cézanne produced portraits, landscapes and figurative work. Often the still life was an exercise showing off the artist's skill as a painter. The scale of the paintings and the time taken to paint them was less than that needed for figure painting. The artist could therefore sell his work for a more modest price allowing it to become available to a wider market. In due course, still life painting was to become a significant activity in European art.

In your examination you will have to answer one question on still life, with Parts A and B. Part A will involve you studying an illustrated example of still life. The work will come from the period you have been studying: 1750 to the present day. It could be in any medium; it may not be a painting but a construction, collage, sculpture or photograph. The means and materials of its production will be given in addition to its size. This information is very important to you when examining the illustration. It will help you interpret and understand what you are looking at.

Generally, the questions will be about composition, technique and use of visual elements or subject matter. You should therefore always consider these things when looking at an artist's work and practising for your exam. Practise giving your opinion and justifying what you have to say. Part A questions are worth 10 marks.

Candidates are asked to discuss the composition of a painting in Part A questions. They are expected to comment on subject matter, use of visual elements and media handling. They should also include their opinion of the painting.

The artist uses colour, tone and composition successfully. The artist has not used a great variety of colours but has mainly used cold colours except from the orange that gives the picture warmth.◄ He has used a very pale beige colour in the background, which is darker under the shelf. He then uses a clear cut white for the objects on the shelf which I feel are interesting because it highlights them from the background.◄ However, he uses a burst of colour through the tin boxes in orange, mint green and purple. I think this has been done well as it makes them very eye catching to the viewer and highlights them from the muted tones of the background.◄ The artist has also used a cream colour on the vase, which separates it from the rest of the crockery.◄

Tone plays a very large part in this painting as the same colour has been used in many parts of the painting and tone is what separates the objects.◄ I particularly like how he has used darker tones for shadows under the shelf, on the sides of the objects etc. I like how these tones give the painting real-life characteristics as if it was a photograph.◄ The artist has also used a lighter tone on the objects to highlight their importance against a slightly darker background.◄

In my opinion it looks amazing how he has brought these objects away from the background by giving them mid tone shadows on the wall. The composition is beautiful. The artist has used a very low straight line (the shelf), which gives the painting height.◄ He then uses the three colourful objects on the left, but keeps them tied in with the white by giving them a dark shadow to contrast with their brightness.

(◄ indicates a point worthy of 1 mark)

This answer is worth 7 or 8 marks. The writer gives an opinion about the composition straight away. The essay discusses the visual elements of colour in some detail and then looks at how tone is used. They speak about composition throughout. Despite this, the analysis is repetitive and quite simplistic. They have not discussed media handling or subject matter. You must be careful to read the question accurately. If you don't and you miss an important part of the question you will not be able to gain full marks.

Part B questions deal with your knowledge of the working methods and practices of renowned artists from the period 1750 to the present day. You will be asked to compare the work of two prominent artists or movements. In Higher they should be from different time periods. You will be expected to have a thorough understanding of their work, the influences on them and their influences on others.

The question may ask you to comment on their choice of subjects, styles or working methods. You may be expected to comment on composition, media handling or use of the visual elements. Up to 16 marks are generally awarded to this part of the answer. A further 4 marks are available for the explanation of the importance of the artists in the development of their chosen field.

Candidates are asked to explain why two artists' still life works are successful. They are asked to refer to examples of the artists work and say why the artists are important in the development of still life. The artists should be from different times or movements.

The two artists I have chosen to compare are Paul Cezanne and Pablo Picasso. Cezanne worked in the Post-Impressionist period beginning in 1885 and his aim in his work was to create 3-D shapes on a 2-D canvas.◄ Picasso worked during the Cubist period, in a style he and Georges Braque developed from Paul Cezanne's ideas, and this began from 1907 onwards.◄ He too wanted to produce 3-D shapes in his work and he did so by breaking objects down into their component geometric shapes and rearranging them.◄

Cezanne, however, drew objects in a fairly realistic manner then distorted them by drawing parts of the object that were not visible from his point of view, but he knew appeared as he drew them.◄

Examples of these similarities and contrasts are obvious in Cezanne's still life composition Apples and Oranges and Picasso's Still Life with a Skull.◄

This piece of Cezanne's is very bright and enthusiastic and he thoroughly exploits the visible phenomenon that warm colours appear to come forward while cool colours recede.◄ This is how he has created a sense of perspective in this piece.◄

Picasso on the other hand has used only two colours, black and white, in his piece. He creates perspective by outlining all the geometric components of the objects and filling in the spaces between shapes in the foreground and leaving blank open spaces to create the background.◄ Cezanne's piece appears realistic at first glance, however, there are some aspects to the placing of the fruit that are not physically possible and some items of fruit are distorted as he has drawn parts of them even if they appear to be hidden by the material they are placed in.◄ Picasso has achieved his 3-D piece by breaking down all the objects into component shapes and rearranging them in a fairly distorted manner.◄

Cezanne was a very influential artist in the way he moved art on from the Impressionist period. He rejected all the crude brushstrokes familiar to that period and created texture and life in his paintings by distorting what he drew.◄ Picasso was heavily influenced by Cezanne and built on what he had started. He didn't just paint slight distortions of what he saw, but completely broke down the objects he was drawing and arranged them to create what he felt was the composition he saw in front of him.◄

(◄ indicates a point worthy of 1 mark)

This answer would be worth 11 or 12 marks. It gives us some information, without going into depth, about the two artists chosen. Although the artists chosen are appropriate, the description of the importance of their work is fairly basic. The writer's discussion of the examples does not really tell us anything about the artists' working methods, techniques or media handling. If these had been discussed it would have helped our understanding of the importance of these artists. The writer did not refer to the impact Cubism was to have on artists following on from Picasso and Braque. A closer reading of the question may have prevented this important part of the answer from being missed.

When practising the activities outlined, you should be mindful of the time available to you in the exam. Part A questions should take around 15 minutes, whereas Part B answers may require about 30 minutes to complete.

Within the period you will be studying we have to consider why artists practised still life. An obvious reason is that some painters, for instance Morandi, were not interested in other subject matter and were content with concentrating mainly on inanimate objects.

Most artists, however, also practised other forms of painting. Chardin, for instance, painted domestic scenes in addition to intimate still lifes.

Giorgio Morandi, Still Life (1946)
oil on canvas 37.5x45.7 cm

Now try this...

a) In your opinion, how successfully has Morandi used colour, tone and composition in this painting? Explain your opinion.

b) Compare and contrast two examples of still life by any two artists. Comment on the different approaches used by the artists.

How to Begin

It is important for you to be able to recognise the work of some of the prominent artists of the period you are studying and it is essential to be able to compare their work in terms of influences and working methods. Begin by selecting two artists who are chronologically apart; one from Post-Impressionism and one from Pop Art, for example.

ACTIVITY

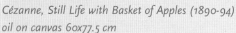

Cézanne, Still Life with Basket of Apples (1890-94) oil on canvas 60x77.5 cm

Douglas Muego, Still Life with Fruit digital print on paper 19 x 18 cm

Carefully study the two works above.

Compare how each of the artists has approached the subject of fruit.

Consider the use of colour, shape, form and use of media.

Which artist's work do you prefer? Explain your judgement.

If you are studying contemporary artists, take care to select those who have achieved some prominence and have had something written about their work. You will then be able to go to a number of sources for information about the artist and their working methods.

If the artist belongs to a specific movement, find out about the movement you have selected and the main characteristics of it. Identify any other artists within the movement who were also engaged in still life painting. Look at examples of their work and select one or two artists whose work you admire. This will allow you to compare the work of your chosen artist with that of others.

Initially when faced with a vast array of books in a library it can be a daunting task knowing where to start. Given that your period of study is 1750 to the present day, you will be faced with a bewildering choice. It is a good idea to choose periods or movements that you have plenty of resources about. Although you may be very keen on a particular painter's work, if you have little or no information about the artist you will find it very difficult to write a good essay on him or her. Remember that, as well as developing your interest in art, you also need to expand your knowledge to be able to pass the exam.

One way we can do this is to look at the period chronologically, noting which of the most important artists were involved in still life. For many of them, still life was not the major focus of their work, but they nevertheless gave it as much importance as the other subjects they painted.

At the beginning of the period you are studying, the artist Chardin was very influential in making still life an acceptable subject in the academic exhibitions of the day. His main interest was in painting everyday objects that could be found in the kitchen.

Probably the earliest group of painters we would consider with relation to still life within the study period would be the Impressionists. The Impressionists' interest in capturing the fleeting moment was expressed best in landscapes and figure compositions. However, artists such as Manet and Fantin-Latour also produced still lifes. Fantin-Latour is noted for producing flower paintings, while Manet was interested in Spanish and Dutch painting and created a number of still lifes at both the beginning and end of his career.

From the main group of Impressionist painters, Pissarro painted quite a few, but Renoir is probably the best known for still life. He painted richly coloured fruit and flower studies in his customary soft focused style.

Renoir, Fruits of the Midi (1881)
oil on canvas 50x65 cm

Now try this...

Look closely at the Renoir still life.

How has the artist used colour and tone throughout the painting?

How has the artist's use of media contributed to the effectiveness of the painting?

How successful has Renoir been in capturing the quality of the vegetables he has painted? Justify your opinions

Cézanne, Still Life with Basket (kitchen table) (1890-95) oil on canvas 65x90 cm

van Gogh, Irises (1890) oil on canvas 92x73 cm

From the Post-Impressionist movement van Gogh is renowned for his various paintings of sunflowers, but Cézanne is the one most associated with still life. He used his still life paintings as a means of experimenting with showing solid objects and their relationship with each other and their surroundings. He also tried applying his theories on the use of colour to show depth within his paintings.

Now try this...

Both of the paintings above were produced at around the same time.

a) Analyse them considering the artists' use of colour, form, tone and space. What do you think each of the artists' main concern was when working on their painting? Which painting do you prefer? Justify your choice.

b) Compare the work of two still life artists from different periods or movements. Discuss the artists' methods, composition and media handling. Why do you think they were important artists?

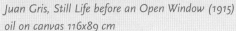

Juan Gris, Still Life before an Open Window (1915)
oil on canvas 116x89 cm

Picasso, Still Life (1914)
painted wood and upholstery fringe 254x457x92 mm

Compare the two Cubist still life works shown above.

Consider the artist's response to the challenge of still life.

Comment on their use of media and composition.

Which of the works do you consider to be most successful? Justify your answer.

Cézanne was an influence on Gauguin and Emile Bernard, but it was the artists Picasso and Braque who took Cézanne's ideas forward in the Cubist movement. Still life was a major subject for Cubist artists. The third great Cubist, Juan Gris, was a major contributor to Synthetic Cubism. He used a greater variety of colour than Picasso and Braque, perhaps influenced by his knowledge of the work of Matisse.

While the Cubists were developing their approaches based on the theories of Cézanne along their own particular direction, Matisse was combining Cézanne's ideas on pictorial structure with Gauguin's use of decorative pattern in a very personal manner. Although most of Matisse's output was concerned with portraying the human figure, he also produced a number of still life works. In many of them he combined decorative flat shapes with large areas of pure colour. He, along with others such as Derain and Dufy, became known as the Fauves, a term given to them due to the extravagant use of pure colour in their paintings.

Matisse, Goldfish and Sculpture (1912)
oil on canvas 116x100 cm

Now try this...

a) Discuss how two or more of the following contribute to the impact of this painting: colour, line, composition and use of media.

b) Compare examples of still life work by two artists from different periods or movements. Comment on the similarities and differences in their choice of subject matter working methods and style.

Later in the twentieth century, a number of artists concerned with movements such as Dada, Surrealism and Pop Art engaged in still life work. Generally it was in the same style as the movements they were associated with.

Georges Braque, The Studio (1939) oil on canvas 113x146 cm

Braque's work echoed the various developments in Cubism and evolved through time. Nolde's paintings were in the Expressionist style and Pop artists such as Roy Lichtenstein and Wayne Thiebaud produced works that fitted in with the thinking of the day. Scottish artists such as the Colourists produced still life paintings as part of their output and, if we visit mixed exhibitions of artists working today, we will see a large number of still life works still being produced.

Remember that not all responses to the theme of still life are paintings. Sculptors and photographers have also produced notable works. Look closely at the following images and consider how the artists approached their subjects.

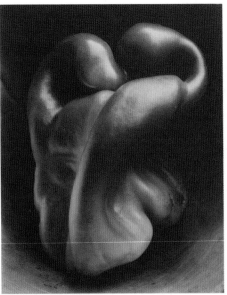

TOP LEFT: *Roy Lichtenstein Sandwich and Soda (1964) silkscreen on mylar 47.5x57.5 cm*

TOP RIGHT: *Samuel John Peploe, Tulips (1923) oil on canvas 61x50 cm*

BOTTOM LEFT: *Alberto Magnelli, Still Life (1914) assemblage: plaster, glass and terra cotta 56x54x56 cm*

BOTTOM RIGHT: *Edward Weston, Pepper No 30 (1930) photographic print 25x18 cm*

ABOVE: *Alberto Morrocco Still Life with Vermillion Vase and Yellow Tile (1996) oil on canvas 71x71 cm*

RIGHT: *Elizabeth Blackadder Two Cats with Clivia (1987) watercolour 76x58 cm*

Study the two paintings above. How has each artist used colour in their composition? How are their stroke technique and approach similar? How are they different?

Exam Preparation

In preparing for your exam you should look in detail at the work of at least **two** different artists or art movements. You should know their background thoroughly, including who may have influenced them. Were they an influence on people who followed on? Were they influential in the development of Still Life? Be sure you can answer these questions thoroughly.

Do not limit your research to a couple of examples from each artist or movement. The better informed you are the more completely you will be able to answer the question paper. Remember that past papers are just a guide to the type of questions that have been asked in previous years. The examiners are always refining the style of question you may be asked. If you have a thorough knowledge of your subject you will be able to respond to changes in questioning.

When looking at still life compositions, we should attempt to understand how the artist approached the work and what his main concerns were. Ask yourself questions like the ones that follow to make sure you are fully prepared.

Who made it? Do you know the name of the artist or anything about them? Having previous knowledge about the artist often helps our appreciation of a piece of artwork.

When was it made? Knowing when the work was made can help our understanding of why it was created. The conditions of the time can have an effect on how the artist approached the task. Technological changes have, throughout history, had an effect on how artists approach their work.

What is the subject matter? Is the work a realistic record of what was seen? Is the response purely accurate or is there an emotional element to it? Try to identify if the artist is concerned with showing the effects of light on the subject. Determine if the effects of light have been intensified to exaggerate form or space in the work, if the viewpoint is important, and if the objects selected have any underlying meaning.

What is the format of the work? What size is it? Decide if it has been made to be viewed in a specific environment. Discover what the work is made from and how the medium has been used. Establish if a particular technique or style of working has been used, and whether it has contributed to the overall effect of the work.

By answering these questions, as well as those you come up with yourself, you will be preparing yourself to give thorough responses on your exam papers.

1.4

The Natural Environment

For the purposes of your Art and Design course, the study of the natural environment can be considered the artist's response to land and seascape. This would include a response to natural occurrences such as the weather and disasters. Depending on where you live, your practical work will either be based on direct observation of the landscape near you or be done from photographic or sketch references. Both approaches can mirror those of artists in the past.

In your examination you will have to answer one full question on the natural environment, with Parts A and B. Part A will involve you analysing an illustrated example from the period you have been studying i.e. 1750 to the present day. It could be in any medium; it may not be a painting, but a construction, collage or photograph. The means and materials of the artwork's production will be given as well as its size. This information is very important to you when examining the illustration. It will help you interpret and understand what you are looking at.

Generally, the questions will be about composition, technique and use of visual elements. You may also be asked about your emotional response to the work, however. Therefore, always consider these things when looking at an artist's work and practising for your exam. Practise giving your opinion on the work and justifying what you have to say, as this will become an important aspect of your responses.

Example Question and Response

Candidates are asked to comment on a piece of sculpture called *Sidewinder* by the artist Andy Goldsworthy. They are asked whether they think it is effective in its setting.

This sculpture by Andy Goldsworthy called Sidewinder is quite interesting. The idea of a sculpture made of wood, to me seems slightly strange, more the fact that he hasn't done much with the wood. It is very natural.◄ The wood doesn't seem to have been sanded rather stripped of all of it's foliage. It is made from wood that has been bent by the wind.◄ The wind, also being a natural element adds to the power of the piece. It is quite large in scale (2x100m) this seems to me quite long and a lot of wood must have gone into making it.◄ As a response to the natural environment it seems quite accomplished, using wood and the effects of the wind on wood.◄ The size of the sculpture is interesting. The name sidewinder seems appropriate as the sculpture winds through the accompanying trees beside the roadside.◄ I think the artist wanted to portray that something made out of these fibres which are all natural should seem natural in the

51

environment. It is quite a modern piece, from 1985. This is obvious as it isn't typical of any previous movement and it appears quite a new and innovative idea.◀ I quite like the title although it reminds me of a song by REM. This is another indication that it is modern. The name is quite different. I am not quite sure about this as a piece of art. I find the ideas behind the sculpture quite clever, using the natural environment to shape the wood, but I find it strange that the piece seems out of place. It seems that a piece of work made out of materials that are around it anyway should fit in better with the landscape which the materials come from. His idea to put the sculpture here must have had something to do with it, but it makes the otherwise natural environment seem unnatural. As though man has come along, uprooted something and ruined what was there.◀

(◀ indicates a point worthy of 1 mark)

This answer is worth about 7 or 8 marks. This person has managed to select the main characteristics of the piece – scale, materials, setting and means of production. Some of the inferences are a little fanciful and their opinion on the success of the piece is a little confused.

Part B questions deal with your knowledge of the working methods and practices of renowned artists from the period 1750 to the present day. You will be asked to compare the work of two prominent artists or movements. In Higher they should be from different time periods. You will be expected to have a thorough understanding of their work, the influences on them and their influences on others.

The question may ask you to comment on their choice of subjects, styles or working methods. You may be expected to comment on composition, media handling or use of the visual elements. Up to 16 marks are generally awarded to this part of the answer. A further 4 marks are available for the explanation of the importance of the artists in the development of their chosen field of work.

Candidates are asked to discuss the work of two artists from different times or movements who have been inspired by the natural environment. Referring to specific examples, they are asked how the artists' work is similar and how it differs. The answer should also explain why they are considered to be important artists.

If Claude Monet is regarded as one of the most important Impressionists then Paul Cezanne should be highly thought of because he learned from Monet and adapted his techniques into his own art.◀

Both Monet and Cezanne rejected the academic ideas of their time. Monet was regarded as the leader of the Impressionist movement and Cezanne was a leading Post-Impressionist, influenced by Impressionism.◀

Just as Monet influenced Cezanne's art, Cezanne's work inspired Pablo Picasso. Picasso actually called Cezanne 'my one and only master'. Cezanne's art became a fundamental influence on the Fauves and the Cubists.◀

Claude Monet liked to paint outdoors exploring the changes of light on his subject at various time of the day, capturing the differences of light, colour and texture.◄ This meant he had to paint quickly in many different weather conditions. He liked to paint haystacks, rivers and water lilies.◄ He was influenced by many people. Eugene Boudin was an important early influence on him. He was a landscape artist who encouraged Monet to paint outdoors in front of his subject. He was also influenced by Manet and Turner, who liked to show light and weather conditions in their paintings.◄

Cezanne's paintings are restricted by his ideas and feelings whereas Monet, with his powerful, ever alert eye, was able to paint brilliantly coloured pictures but also with natural tones. He was very reactive to what he saw.◄

Cezanne loved colour as much as Manet but used it in a very different way. His brushstrokes were long and sure whereas Monet's were short daubs of colour. Cezanne had developed his own individual and systematic technique, using flat brushes to create parallel strokes of paint.◄ He aimed to create a balance of colour in his paintings. He tried to do this by eliminating lines, trying to make colour replace drawing. This created an effect of fullness in the painting.◄ He loved the geometry of his paintings and liked to think of all nature as a series of cones, spheres and cylinders.◄ His earlier style was the complete opposite. It was rough, unrefined a riot of thick brushstrokes and colour, of passionate, even somewhat erotic themes. This contrasted with the bland smooth brushstrokes muted colour and lofty subject matter of the academic artists of the time.◄

Cezanne developed an accurate representation of texture and light, with colours placed on the canvas using simultaneous contrast in such a way as to appear in harmony to the eye.◄

Over the years Monet's art underwent a gradual transformation. In his early years he painted a great variety of directly seen subjects. In later years, once he had constructed his enormous garden at Giverny, that would surround him as he worked, he conceived a group of paintings that would surround the viewer in the same way.◄ One of these paintings is called Water Lilies: Green Reflections (1912–1916). It is a close up of a pond's surface. It looks as if you are hovering above the striking colours of purple and greens from the reflections on the water. Monet's handling of paint is loose and fluid and the flowers are indicated with short strokes of paint.◄ The scene of the lightened pond surface creates a sense of movement in the painting.

Monet was determined to finish off his group of 19 canvasses of water lilies as a gift to France, even after he had developed diminished sight. They were completed and hung in L'Orangerie in 1927.◄

Cezanne's style was steadied by the influence of Pissarro. His colours became subdued earth colours rather than the blacks, whites and reds of earlier works. His style was still different from Monet's.◄ Monet's brush strokes were rounded and soft, Cezanne's were longer blunt and more structural. Where Monet was interested in light and colour, Cezanne was more concerned with form and structure.◄ Cezanne invented space in paintings. He used flatness and three-dimensional shape in his paintings. Using both accounted for a distortion of objects and perspective we sometimes see in his work.◄

One of Cezanne's final paintings was called La Montagne Sainte Victorie. The painting uses short brush strokes and bright colours and measures 78x99cm.

He painted this mountain sixty times between 1896 and 1898.◄

(◄ indicates a point worthy of 1 mark)

An excellent response worth full marks. The early paragraphs establish who the writer is discussing and draws comparisons between them right from the beginning. The fact that they were each influential is also established at the beginning of the essay. This explains their importance.

Although they lived close in time they are certainly regarded as being from different movements. Both their inspiration and working methods are then discussed, which points out the similarities and differences of the chosen artists.

Bellini, The Agony in the Garden (1465) egg tempera on wood 81.3x127 cm

When practicing the activities outlined, you should be mindful of the time available to you in the exam. Part A questions should take around 15 minutes, whereas Part B answers will require about 30 minutes.

The study of the natural environment in its own right is quite a recent event in Art History. In the past, landscape was not regarded as a separate type of art or of being worthy of great merit.

If we look back over the history of art, early examples of artistic approaches to the natural environment are shown as background to works of a religious or historical nature. Jan Van Eyck's *The Virgin of Chancellor Rolin*, Bellini's *The Agony in the Garden* and Poussin's *Landscape with St John in Patmos* each show religious scenes where the main subjects of the paintings are seen against idealised landscape backgrounds.

These background landscapes usually show a subjective response to the world around us. They portray scenes that help tell the story of the painting, rather than showing a particular place. Artists today still sometimes change what they see in order to achieve a better composition.

Artists have always made notes or sketches of aspects of nature they have seen in order to inform their finished work. Dürer's watercolour *The Large Turf* and Leonardo da Vinci's *A Rocky Ravine* are examples of pieces created by the artist while actually in the natural environment. This is in contrast to most works painted in the time leading up to the nineteenth century, which were created in the studio from imagination or from memory.

Apart from providing a background to figurative paintings, landscapes record man's impact on nature. They show how towns, houses, farming and industry have affected the land. Bruegel's *The Harvesters* and Constable's *Wivenhoe Park* are excellent examples of this.

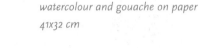

ABOVE: *Dürer, The Large Turf (1503) watercolour and gouache on paper 41x32 cm*

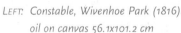

LEFT: *Constable, Wivenhoe Park (1816) oil on canvas 56.1x101.2 cm*

In more recent years, some artists have become involved in commenting on man's responsibilities with regard to ecological change or environmental pollution. Some, such as Andy Goldsworthy, integrate the artwork into the landscape, using natural materials found at the site of their work. In order to better appreciate the works produced by artists who represent the natural environment we should consider the artistic difficulties and constraints on the artist.

The depiction of space and distance would come high on a list of problems faced by artists. The portraitist or still life artist can construct a work with quite a shallow depth of field. The subject can satisfactorily be shown in front of a wall or drape that is close to the picture plane. In a land or seascape, however, the depth of the scene may need to recede to a distant horizon.

One of the techniques used to convey a feeling of distance for the spectator is to show the scene from a high viewpoint. This allows the viewer to look down on the scene shown. An example of this is Pissarro's *The Rainbow*.

Pissarro, The Rainbow (1877)
oil on canvas 53x81 cm

This painting places the viewer on a rise looking down upon a collection of farmhouses with the landscape unfolding towards a distant horizon. Sometimes paintings that use a high viewpoint also show a winding path or river, which take the eye from the foreground into the distance.

Now try this...

Find examples by two artists from different periods that have used a high viewpoint in their paintings. Describe what is shown in the works.

How successfully have the artists shown distance by using this technique?

Another technique used to convey distance is aerial perspective. The artist uses diminishing tonal values: the strongest tones are in the foreground, gradually fading in the middle distance, and palest tones showing the features furthest away.

Caspar David Friedrich, The Solitary Tree (1822)
oil on canvas 55x71 cm

Now try this...

With a partner, gather a selection of four or more images in which artists have used fading tones to portray recession. Make your selection from nineteenth and twentieth century artists and photographers.

Prepare an illustrated talk with your partner, highlighting the importance of the artists' approach to the natural environment.

Contrasting colour is also used effectively in aerial perspective. The warmest colours, such as browns, reds and yellows, are in the foreground, with greens in the middle distance, and cooler blues and purples on the horizon. These devices can give a great feeling of depth in a work.

Almost as important as the treatment of the land or sea is the way in which the artist paints the sky. Constable was a painter who devoted much time to the study of clouds and sky, producing many sketches and paintings of cloud formations and differing light effects. Turner also made remarkable use of skies in both his land and seascape paintings. Sometimes they are peaceful and calm, while on other occasions are dark and brooding. They give the scene a life and vigour due to an often dramatic use of light.

Now try this...

a) Discuss the methods used by Turner to produce this response to nature. Comment on his use of colour tone and media handling. How successful has Turner been in capturing the power of the elements?

b) Discuss the work of two artists from different periods who have been inspired by the natural environment. Explain the methods used by them to create mood or atmosphere in their response to nature.

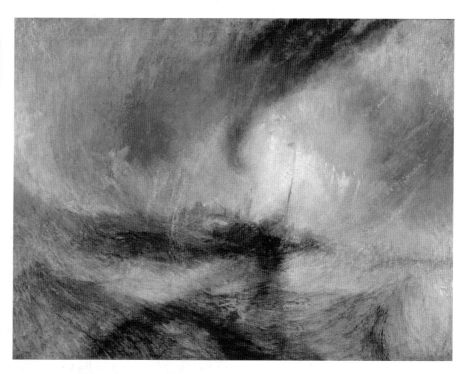

Turner, Snow Storm – Steam-Boat off a Harbour's Mouth (1842) oil on canvas 91.4x121.9cm

Landscape as a separate art form developed in Holland in the seventeenth century. After the Reformation, when religious painting went out of favour, artists in Northern Europe began to look to other subject areas for their paintings. People in Holland at the time were interested in the observation of fact, which helped lead Dutch artists to develop landscape as a theme. With its expanding commercial market, Holland was becoming an important trading nation and its citizens wanted a record of their commercial success. Rich merchants began buying in the newly developing art market. Although wealthy, these new collectors

Canaletto, A Regatta on the Grand Canal (1740)
oil on canvas 22.1x182.8 cm

were generally not educated in a classical tradition. Their interest was not in the classical landscapes of Nicholas Poussin or Claude Lorraine, but in art that reflected pride in their developing nation and the prosperity it was enjoying. Landscapes by artists such as Jacob van Ruysdael, showing local scenes and events, satisfied this want. Portraiture, paintings of domestic scenes, still life and landscape became the main focus for artists at this time.

Traditionally, the opinion was that landscape should be idealistic rather than naturalistic. Rules of what made a good landscape were developed by the Artistic Academies. Artists, particularly at the beginning of their careers, who wanted public approval for their work needed to successfully exhibit in the academy exhibitions in their countries. To gain entry to academy exhibitions they generally accepted the rules then in force. Even up until the 1850s, artists like Corot were following such rules in order to gain acceptance for their work e.g. *Dance of the Nymphs* in which he shows a group of figures dancing within an idealised landscape.

Corot, La Danse des Nymphes (1850)
oil on canvas 38.5x51.25 inches

Although the landscape is the main focus of the painting, Corot felt he needed to include the figures in order that the work gain acceptance by the Academy. Later, his work was to become more realistic in its appearance.

Landscapes were traditionally produced in the artist's studio. The advantage of this being that the picture could be developed over a long period. The disadvantage, of course, was that the work was not a direct response to nature but a view based on memory and reflection. Consequently, many artists adopted (and continue to use) the practice of sketching outside in front of a view. The mediums used vary from pencil to crayon to watercolour, the sketch typically being done on a small scale. These notes are then taken back to the studio to be developed later. Although this is a practical approach, it interrupts the artist's direct visual contact with the subject.

Sam Bough, In Glen Massan (1856)

The artist Constable built his compositions up gradually following a series of individual studies of elements he wished to include. He made studies of trees, buildings, clouds etc. directly from nature that were later composed into a variety of sketches done within his studio. It was only after this process that he arrived at the final paintings. For his large exhibition paintings, his 'six footers', Constable found that the small sketches he had used to build up his compositions were not sufficient. Instead, he painted full-size sketches.

Some people prefer the spontaneous paint handling of Constable's sketches to the more worked final paintings. However, Constable never exhibited them. His later 'six footers' became looser in paint handling as he used a palette knife to build up pigment and define forms; a practice he had begun to use on his full-size sketches.

Although very realistic looking, his work is rarely an accurate description of a particular scene. Rather, Constable composes views that sum up his experience of a particular place. His great rival Turner also carefully sketched small studies of places he had seen on his travels. Turner, however, did not gradually build up the final compositions of his paintings. His paintings are more an emotional response to a theme, inspired by something seen, then developing into an imaginative work.

Now try this...

Compare the work of two artists or movements you have looked at that make skies an important element in their paintings.

What mood or effect are they trying to achieve?

How successful have they been?

Give examples to illustrate your opinions.

In the nineteenth century the Impressionists were among the first groups to work directly from nature. The development of transport in the mid nineteenth century allowed easy access to the countryside, and the introduction of tube paints made working on canvas directly from nature much easier than it had previously been. The need to transport the canvasses, however, limited the size that the artists could easily work upon. Many of the works done in the field are quite small in size.

Monet was so intent on directly recording his response to the scene that he went to the extent of having a boat set up as a studio from which he could observe the changing effects of light and reflections on water. He worked quickly, swapping canvasses as the light changed, trying to retain as accurate a feeling of what he was seeing as was possible. Working quickly over short periods of time caused the artists to use the short, broken brush strokes that became a characteristic of Impressionism.

Monet, The Water-Lily Pond (1899)
oil on canvas 88.3x93.1 cm

The newly available, chemically-produced paint colours were also a great asset to the Impressionist painters. These were much brighter than natural colours and allowed the painters to more easily portray the effects of light. Monet's final attempts to paint directly from nature saw him construct a studio within his garden at Giverny that he had developed as a source of inspiration for his paintings of water lilies.

Now try this...

> Discuss the subject and composition of Monet's *Water Lily Pond*. Comment on the artist's use of colour and shape. Explain your personal reaction to this work.

Impressionism, with its emphasis on capturing the fleeting moment, did not satisfy all of the artists involved in the movement. Cézanne, who had been encouraged in his experiments with Impressionism by Pissarro, began to find its theories too limiting. He started to study the underlying structure of what he saw in an attempt to make his paintings more solid looking. Cézanne observed, 'Everything in nature adheres to the cone, the cylinder and the cube'. This observation caused him to develop a style of almost geometric-looking pictures that he built up slowly with short rectangular brushstrokes. In his landscape paintings, Cézanne responded directly to the countryside around Aix-en-Provence where he lived. In his case, the nearby mountain, Mont St. Victoire was to become a recurring theme in his work. He painted a series of pictures of the mountain that show not only his love for a particular spot, but his involvement in painting as a formal exercise. When looking at his paintings he makes us aware that a painting is just that; he does not try to trick the eye, but produces a work in which we are aware of the arrangement of painted marks on a flat surface. Cézanne's analysis of form was to be further developed by the Cubists.

Cézanne's contemporary, Vincent van Gogh, developed an equally personal style of painting. In his case, he used longer swirling brush strokes with which to capture the scene. Paintings such as *The Starry Night* or *The Olive Grove* (both 1889) seem to dance across the canvas, with their twisting brushstrokes of thick intense pigment giving the work an expressive quality not seen before.

Paul Cézanne, The Bay from L'Estaque (1886)
oil on canvas 31.5x38.5 inches

Vincent van Gogh, *Wheat Field with Cypresses* (1889) oil on canvas 72.5x91.5 cm

In reassessing the place of painting in a world in which photography was becoming more prominent as an art form, twentieth century artists developed new views as to the formal aspects of painting. Picasso and Braque, in developing Cubism, looked upon landscape painting as providing a frame in which to explore ideas about viewpoint, ways of seeing or composition. They were to take the ideas advanced by Cézanne and develop them further into a new way of viewing the world. For a time their paintings were remarkably alike. Braque's *Viaduct at L'Estaque* (1908) and Picasso's *Landscape with a Bridge* (1909) show a clear link with the work of Cézanne and could almost have been painted by the same hand.

BELOW RIGHT: *Georges Braque, Viaduct at L'Estaque* (1908) oil on canvas 72.5x59 cm

BELOW LEFT: *Pablo Picasso, Landscape with a Bridge* (1909) oil on canvas 81x100 cm

Later in the twentieth century, Scottish artists Peploe and Fergusson, who had been influenced first by The Glasgow Boys, and later by advances in artistic thinking taking place in France, were to develop a style of painting that brought together some of the structural aspects of early Cubism with a much more vivid palette. They were to become known, along with Hunter and Cadell, as The Scottish Colourists. Although many of their landscape paintings were of the Scottish countryside, their concern with the arrangements of their compositions and fresh use of colour was to make them influential.

In the twentieth century landscape painting was to remain popular with many artists. Their focus, however, changed in line with other developments in art. For some, the boundaries between abstraction and figuration became blurred. The style of work produced ranged from expressive, forceful painting echoing the moods of the weather and times of day to balanced compositions based on a memory of something seen.

F B Cadell, North Wind, Iona (The Bather)
oil on panel 36.8x45 cm

Now try this...

LEFT: *Charles Rennie Mackintosh, The Village of La Lagonne*

ABOVE: *Prunella Clough, Geological Landscape (1949)*
lithograph on paper 14.9x20.1 cm

a) What are the main differences between the two responses to the natural environment illustrated above? Consider the artists' working methods in your answer.

b) Discuss the work of two artists from different movements or periods who have taken inspiration from the natural environment. Giving examples, comment on their working methods and styles. State why they are seen as important artists.

Edward Weston, Juniper, Lake Tenya (1937) gelatine silver print 24.2x19.3 cm

PHOTOGRAPHY

Many of the early advances in landscape photography were by photographers employed by national governments. These images were used to record their colonial expansion or enterprising businesses employed in developing new transport links or territories. The photographer's concern was therefore to provide a visual survey of the lands in which they travelled.

Others, such as Carleton Watkins, were so impressed by the scale of the country that he felt compelled to convey his impressions to others. In order to do this he had a camera made large enough to take 18 by 22 inch negatives, allowing him to print large-scale images that showed in detail the grandeur of the American West. In contrast to this, Edward Weston was to look at the natural environment in great detail producing striking images of often overlooked aspects of nature.

Weston's friend Ansel Adams was to produce the most striking images of North America. Not only did he capture the scale and grandeur of the area, but the careful composition and balance of his photographs show America in an almost romantic light and as an ideal land. It was with this aesthetic that Adams used a collection of his images in 1936, including that of Mount Clarence King, to convince Secretary of the Interior Harold Ickes to protect the Sierra Nevada mountain range in California. Within four years, the area was set aside as Kings Canyon National Park. In addition to his wilderness preservation efforts, Adams' legacy is that he significantly helped raise the art of photography to a level equal with other art forms, such as painting and sculpture, and highlighted the ability of a photograph to convey strong emotion and beauty.

Ansel Adams, Mount Clarence King (1936) gelatine silver print

LAND ART

For some artists the involvement with the environment involves them altering it directly. It was popular in America in the 1960s and 1970s where among its most famous practitioners were Christo, Walter de Maria and Robert Smithson. In the UK, prominent figures are Richard Long, Andy Goldsworthy and Chris Drury. One of the common aims of land artists has been to make us re-evaluate our place in the world, to look at it differently and to consider the planet's place in the universe.

Smithson's most famous work is Spiral Jetty, a spiralling construction 450 meters long stretching out into Great Salt Lake. This huge undertaking involved moving hundreds of tons of earth and rock, but its scale is so great it can only really be appreciated from the air.

Christo's approach has also been on a grand scale. His technique is to wrap areas of land such as Central Park in New York City and islands in Biscayne Bay, Florida with various materials. By obscuring the detail of the area, Christo offers us a new way to interact with our surroundings. Because of the technique involved, his work has only remained for a limited time and we now access it through photographic records and notes.

Richard Long made some of his early works by walking repeated paths over the same stretch of land – the resulting marks being the artwork. Many of his gallery or site-specific pieces involve transporting pieces of stone or found wood to a site and re-assembling them there into some sort of pattern or arrangement. All of these works are meant to represent a 'distillation of experience' and nourish the imagination.

Andy Goldsworthy's sculpture is varied in scale and in the type of materials he uses. His more permanent sculptures have been made of stone, clay or wood. Once constructed, they may be left in the landscape to be discovered by people travelling through at a later date. In many pieces he uses very fragile materials such as ice, twigs and even leaves and flowers to make the sculptures. Because of this they are of a temporary nature and soon after being made deteriorate and eventually disappear. The processes of growth, existence and decay are all part of the work. The photographic recording of the sculpture is very much part of the process as it is the only record that the work was ever made.

Exam Preparation

In preparing for your exam you should look in detail at the work of at least **two** different artists or art movements. You should know their background thoroughly, including who may have influenced them. Were they an influence on people who followed on? Were they influential in the development of responses to The Natural Environment? Be sure you can answer these questions thoroughly.

Do not limit your research to a couple of examples from each artist or movement. The better informed you are the more completely you will be able to answer the question paper. Remember that past papers are just a guide to the type of questions that have been asked in previous years. The examiners are always

TOP: *Robert Smithson, Spiral Jetty (1970)*

MIDDLE: *Christo, Surrounded Island (1983)*

BOTTOM: *Andy Goldsworthy (2005)*

refining the style of question you may be asked. If you have a thorough knowledge of your subject you will be able to respond to changes in questioning.

When looking at work based on the natural environment we should attempt to understand how the artist approached the work and what his main concerns were. Ask yourself questions like the ones that follow to make sure you are fully prepared.

Who made it? Do you know the name of the artist or anything about them? Having previous knowledge about the artist often helps our appreciation of a piece of artwork.

When was it made? Knowing when the work was made can help our understanding of why it was created. The conditions of the time can have an effect on how the artist approached the task. Technological changes have, throughout history, had an effect on how artists approach their work.

What is the subject matter? Is the work a realistic record of a place? Is the response purely accurate or is there an emotional element to it? Try to identify if the artist is concerned with depicting the power of nature. Determine if the artist is interested in showing us the effects of light on the scene, and if these effects of light have been intensified to exaggerate form or space in the work. Ask, also, if the season or time of day is important.

What is the format of the work? What size is it? Decide if it has been made to be viewed in a specific environment. Discover what the work is made from and how the medium has been used. Establish if a particular technique or style of working has been used, and whether it has contributed to the overall effect of the work.

By answering these questions, as well as those you come up with yourself, you will be preparing yourself to give thorough responses on your exam papers.

1.5

The Built Environment

Producing practical work under the heading of The Built Environment presents many of the same challenges as Figure Composition and Portraiture. Often, you will be working from drawings and photographs of buildings and architecture. Ideally, these structures will be local to you so that you have a chance to visit them first hand. You might also find yourself working outside, making drawings and studies of the area you are interested in interacting with. Through this interaction you will begin to develop responses that may take the form of site-specific construction, sculpture, painting, photography or video.

Like portraiture and figure composition, working with the built environment requires you to decide the format you will work in. What materials will allow you to best express your ideas? Will you be painting with watercolour or using thick impasto? If using dry media such as crayons or chalks will you allow the marks of the drawing medium show or will you blend your colours and tones?

Will you be happy with one medium or will you use mixed media, perhaps printing or collage? How will the proportions of scale of your work contribute to its overall effectiveness? Will it be small and intimate encouraging the viewer to get close and examine the detail carefully, or will it be big and bold, best taken in from a distance?

If you have been considering these sorts of questions in relation to your own work you will have been doing the same thing as the famous artists whose work you will be studying as part of your Art Studies unit. When you look at their work, ask yourself these same questions in relation to it. This will help you gain a better understanding of the artists' intentions, and in turn inspire and help you with your own work.

In your Art Studies, you are preparing yourself for the written exam. Part A questions will involve you studying an illustrated example of a piece of artwork fitting the description of The Built Environment. The work will come from the period you have been studying i.e. 1750 to the present day. It could be in any medium; it may not be a painting, but a collage, sculpture or photograph. The means and materials of the work's production will be given in addition to its size. This information is very important to you when examining the illustration. It will help you interpret and understand what you are looking at.

Generally, the questions in Part A will be about composition, technique and use of visual elements. You may also be asked to comment on the significance of the theme, as well as the emotional response you have on viewing the work. These elements, therefore, should always be considered when looking at an artist's work and practising for your exam. Practise giving your opinion and justifying what you have to say, as this will frequently be asked as well.

Question A asks candidates to respond to a painting by Sir Robin Philipson of a cathedral interior. They are asked to refer to at least two of the following: colour, shape, pattern and composition. They are also asked their opinion of the painting.

I feel that Sir Robin Philipson's painting of Cathedral Interior (1978) is highly colourful with a rather complex and interesting composition.◄ This oil on canvas is very striking in colour; I personally feel that these colours would not often be seen in an ordinary cathedral.◄ Perhaps the colours are supposed to represent the colours that show through the coloured patterned glass window.◄ The main colour in this work is yellow. I think this may represent that this cathedral like many others is a place of happiness where people have no worries; a holy place.◄ There is a great use of pattern throughout. To the right there are straight vertical lines of block colour, I feel that this sort of pattern doesn't really relate to a cathedral more a carnival or circus.◄ I feel this painting has many delicate and detailed parts, like the top right hand side, the column.◄ However, I feel that when looking at this as a whole it's rather complicated – the subject matter isn't clear until you read the title of the whole.◄ I think Philipson was painting the atmosphere of the cathedral rather than the interior. I feel this painting has warmth to it; however, the composition of the blue arch in the centre has a cold feel to it.◄

(◄ indicates a point worthy of 1 mark)

This is a good response worth about 8 marks. The writer has mentioned colour, composition and pattern. The inferences drawn are intelligent and show some understanding of the concerns of the artist. A more in-depth discussion of composition, analysing the balance of shapes, or more detailed consideration of the effects of pattern would have gained full marks. Could you add to the answer in order to gain the maximum marks?

Part B questions deal with your knowledge of the working methods and practices of renowned artists from the period 1750 to the present day. You will be asked to compare the work of two prominent artists or movements. In Higher they should be from different time periods. You will be expected to have a thorough understanding of their work, the influences on them and their influences on others.

The question may ask you to comment on their choice of subjects, styles or working methods. You may be expected to comment on composition, media handling or use of the visual elements. Up to 16 marks are generally awarded to this part of the answer. A further 4 marks are available for the explanation of the importance of the artists in the development of their chosen field of work.

Question B asks candidates to discuss the work of two artists based on the built environment, explaining their working methods. They are asked to give typical examples of each artist's work.

Two artists I have been studying are Claude Monet of the Impressionist movement and LS Lowry, an English artist who lived in the twentieth century. Monet was famous for painting with broken brush strokes and Lowry was famous for his 'stick men'. Although both painted buildings and the city their paintings are very different.◄ Monet lived in France between 1840 and 1926 and is famous for being the founder of Impressionism. Impressionist artists worked outside studying the effects of light on what they were painting.◄ Because light is always changing they did a lot of paintings (series) of the same thing to show how it was different at different times or seasons.◄ One famous series of Monet's was of Rouen cathedral.◄ He painted it over twenty-five times from the same spot, but the paintings are all different because the light moved across the front of the cathedral making different shadows as it moved.◄ Monet painted the shadows in complementary colours, a technique used by the Impressionists.◄ He also used short brushstrokes of colour dabbed onto the canvas. This was because he had to work quickly as the light was changing.◄ This is very true in the version I was studying, Rouen Cathedral: Harmony in Blue and Gold.◄ In this painting Monet uses thick impasto to build up layers of colour. Most of the front of the cathedral is painted in yellows and the shadows are purple — the complementary colour of yellow.◄ The front of the church fills up most of the painting with just a little blue sky at the top. Another series Monet painted in the city was of the Gare Saint-Lazare, a railway station he used in Paris. They were also painted in the Impressionist style.◄

LS Lowry was born in Manchester in 1887 and died in 1976. Most of his life he lived in Manchester, working as a rent collector and painting at night.◄ Most of his paintings were of the city around Salford where he worked. They show factory buildings and the terrace houses where the workers lived.◄ A lot of them show crowds of people going to or from work or just in the street.◄ Whenever he went Lowry drew. If he did not have a sketchbook he drew on any scraps of paper that were handy.◄ A lot of his drawings were of people he saw as he walked around collecting rent. He later used them in his paintings.◄ Lowry also did paintings of the coast near Berwick on Tweed where he went on holiday nearly every year. Lowry's paintings were done on canvas that he first painted white.◄ He left them for a while in his studio and let the white turn cream before beginning to paint. He did not use many colours in his paintings, just white, black, red, blue and dull yellow.◄ They were enough to show the city and the factories covered in soot. He painted the people with long smooth brushstrokes that made them look like stick people.◄

An example of Lowry's painting that I studied is called Canal and Factories painted in 1955.◄ It shows just what the title says along with people walking in the street. There are some boats on the canal and smoke coming from the factory chimneys. The people's houses are small beside the factories that are painted grey. It is a very typical painting of Lowry's.◄

(◄ indicates a point worthy of 1 mark)

This is a good response worth full marks. In the first paragraph the writer names the artists he is going to be discussing. The second section of the essay describes Monet's working methods and gives examples of his work, appropriate to the theme and typical of an Impressionist approach. The next section does the same for Lowry. The essay covers all points asked for in the question.

The built environment is often considered to be a part of landscape painting rather than a theme on its own. Cities, towns or prominent buildings have long been a part of paintings, usually as a background to figurative or landscape subjects. However, around the second half of the seventeenth century paintings of town or cityscapes became popular in Holland and Italy. They usually showed specific buildings or views, rather than imaginary ones, which was often the case when used as background for figurative paintings. They commonly were bought by travellers as souvenirs, or were commissioned by civic groups proud of a new building or development. The paintings generally show a well-ordered civic scene with accurately drawn buildings and ordered small groups of people going about their business. This format remained the case for many years.

Within the time frame of your course, Canaletto (1697–1765) is the earliest painter to specialise in portraying the city. Although his finest work was at the beginning of his career, he continued to be popular, especially with British collectors, producing a steady stream of works. His success was such that he needed to employ a number of studio assistants to produce enough work to satisfy the demands of his buyers. Despite these demands, Canaletto insisted on producing well-balanced compositions, not just copies of popular views. In achieving the accuracy that is a feature of his work, he may have used a camera obscura (an optical device like a large pinhole camera that projected a view of the outside world on to a surface allowing an artist to accurately trace it).

Neoclassical artists such as David or Ingres depict an historical setting in many of their paintings, using devices such as classically inspired columns or arches to suggest settings for the work. The background is sometimes ambiguous, in so far as it could be an indoor or outdoor setting that is being shown. The scale of the buildings and the quality of the architecture shown tends to suggest grand buildings, that we would expect to find in urban environments. The buildings, however, are not the subjects of the paintings; they are intended to assist the telling of the story of the work.

Artists of the Romantic Movement are similar in that respect, their paintings were generally inspired by events in literature or history and any reference to a built environment is usually as a background to a particular story. When urban scenes are depicted, the Impressionists are usually accurate in the perspectives of the buildings they show. However, they were primarily concerned with the effect of light on the scene and developing their ideas about picture composition. Living at a time when cities were developing in response to social changes, the Impressionists wanted to show modern life around them. In their paintings, the busy crowds and inhabitants of the cities are as important as the buildings.

William Simpson, The Trongate (1849)
oil on canvas

Now try this...

Find examples by two artists who have used the built environment as a source of inspiration and who use crowds to people the scenes.

How successful do you think they have been in representing a busy place? Do their works seem more convincing because of the crowds? Are any of the people in the works recognisable characters? Justify your choice.

The built environment rarely features work by the Post-Impressionists; when buildings are shown they are generally seen in rural settings. One of the few exceptions is Cézanne's *Gardanne* where the artist shows the huddle of buildings built around the hillside in the village.

Now try this...

Sisley, Moret-sur-Loing (1891) oil on canvas 65x92 cm

Cézanne, Gardanne (1885-86) oil on canvas 65x100 cm

Compare the composition of the two paintings by Sisley and Cézanne shown above.

In your response discuss at least two of the following: *colour, tone, perspective, shape.*

Which painting do you consider to be most successful?

Between 1904 and 1908 the Fauves, Matisse, Derain and Vlaminck were producing paintings of their surroundings that were nearly abstract. Their primary interest was in using colour in a new way. Matisse had tried using the colour theories of the Neo-impressionist Seurat, but the muted results that were achieved when using these scientific-based theories did not satisfy Matisse. Instead, his choice of colours was based on observation and feeling. The brushwork was bold, using large unblended strokes of colour, producing images that were not intended to mimic the real world. Instead, although the drawing of the scene would be recognisable, the colour ranges used often contained complementary pairings with primary colours included in order to increase the dramatic effect the artist was aiming for.

Although the movement existed only for a short time, it attracted some other artists; Braque regarded his experiments with Fauvism as being important in his development as an artist, while Bonnard was to employ many of their techniques throughout his life.

Derain, St Paul's from the Thames (1906)
oil on canvas 100x82 cm

Now try this...

With a partner, gather a selection of 4 or more images in which artists have dealt with aspects of the built environment. Make your selection from the period 1900 until now.

Prepare your findings in the form of an illustrated talk or brochure, highlighting the importance of the artists' contribution to the theme The Built Environment.

Inspired by the Fauves, the Cubist's main concern when painting the built environment was with formal geometric qualities. The buildings in their paintings were seen as quite abstract shapes with little architectural detail.

When they show the built environment in their work, Expressionist artists usually use it as a background to their main subject, people. An exception to this would be George Grosz, much of whose work is of a political nature and comments on the night life of the city and the deterioration he saw in German society during the inter-war years. Another, whose work shows an interest in architecture, is Lyonel Feininger. Much of Feininger's work was as a cartoonist but his interest changed to painting in a style influenced by Cubism.

Now try this...

Compare the work of two artists from different times or movements you have studied that make the theme The Built Environment an important aspect of their work.

How successful do you think they have been in showing our cities and towns? Have any of them made you look at the way we live in a different light? Give examples to back up your opinions.

Georges Braque, Viaduct at L'Estaque (1908)
73x60 cm

One of the most accomplished painters of the built environment in the early and mid twentieth century was the American artist Edward Hopper. His realistic style of painting America's cities and suburbia has a strong psychological impact, suggesting the emptiness and loneliness felt by many living there. He was a master of capturing atmosphere both at night and under strong sunlight.

The built environment has been a continuing theme used by British artists throughout the twentieth century. The Scottish Colourists recorded their surroundings in the south of France and at home in Scotland.

LEFT:

Robert Delaunay, Champ de Mars: The Red Tower (1911–23) oil on canvas 160x128 cm

BELOW:

Edward Hopper, Nighthawks (1942) oil on canvas 76x152 cm

In the mid century, painters such as Eric Ravilious, John Piper and Edward Bawden who had been involved in producing works for the Festival of Britain continued to look to architecture as a theme.

Artists associated with Pop Art in the 1960s were to reflect on all aspects of their surroundings as their working lives progressed. Pop (short for propaganda) art responded to the social and cultural conditions of the time. In both Britain and the United States, these issues included racism and segregation, consumerism, gender inequality and war. Much of this work incorporated images and themes from popular culture in order to create representational pieces. The built environment was an important aspect of this for many artists.

David Hockney has shown various aspects of the built environment in his work. When he first visited America his fascination with his new environment was recorded in a number of paintings and prints of California. Later, during the period when he was experimenting with photography, he produced numerous studies of architectural settings. These works, made by assembling a collection of details taken from a scene, can require a number of days taking the individual photographs that are used in the final composition. This is in contrast with normal practice where a photograph is taken in a matter of moments.

ABOVE: *Samuel John Peploe, Evening, North Berwick (1905) oil on board 323x41 cm*

Hockney, Place Furstenberg: Paris August 7, 8, 9, 1985 photographic collage 88x80 cm

Now try this...

How successful has David Hockney been in portraying this area of Paris? Refer to colour mood and composition in your response.

Compare the work of two twentieth century artists who have responded to the built environment. Explain their importance using examples of their work to illustrate your opinions.

Though the approaches and techniques used by fantasy artists are rich and varied, we can identify a common ground. Distortion, exaggeration, changes in scale, setting transformation, juxtaposition (putting contrasting objects together), assemblage, realism and abstraction are all common elements throughout the genre.

As a general rule, expect Part A questions to have something unusual in the sources and approaches used by the artists, the materials used or the placement of the work. In Part B questions on fantasy and imagination you should combine your knowledge of the sources and approaches of individual artists with specific historical knowledge of movements, styles and the influences that artists have on each other.

These questions require historical knowledge combined with the skills of critical evaluation. This means that you have to be aware of the historical context of the artists and have knowledge of the characteristics of any art movement to which they belonged. However, by their very nature, some artists associated with fantasy and imagination such as William Blake, Marc Chagall, Henri Rousseau, Maurice Escher, Paul Klee and Edward Burra don't fit easily into any recognisable movement. This should not put you off since their approaches and sources are similar to other artists who belong to movements associated with this theme. By being aware of which artists transcend genre, you should be able to give examples that show a clear contrast of style, and an awareness of different movements and periods required for Part B questions.

There are a number of very popular artists whose work fits easily into fantasy and imagination. The Surrealists are perhaps the most popular, as most if not all of the distinctive features of fantasy and imagination can be found in their work. Surrealist artists can be used in just about any Part B question on this theme, so it is a good idea to spend time becoming familiar with them. They are also a group of artists whose weird imagery appeals to young people.

> **TIP**
>
> *Before selecting artists you should try to acquire a broad overview of the knowledge and historical context of fantasy and imagination. When you understand what the theme is about, you can add depth to your study by further research on individual artists and movements. As with other themes, it is a good idea to focus your preparation on at least two artists clearly identified with the theme.*

Example Question and Answer

Compare examples of work by two artists from different periods or movements. Discuss the approaches and sources used by the artists to communicate their ideas on the theme of fantasy and imagination. Explain why you think they are important examples of this theme.

The two artists that I am going to compare are the Belgian Surrealist artist Rene Magritte and the Irish-born artist Francis Bacon. Both artists are associated with the theme of fantasy and imagination and both use different approaches to communicating their ideas. By comparing the sources and approaches of each artist, I am going to show how each made an important contribution to the development of fantasy and imagination.◄

Francis Bacon was born in Ireland in 1909. As a child, Bacon's family moved around a lot. Later in life he was known as impulsive. This may explain why there is a feeling of displacement in his work.◄

Bacon painted very violent and frightening images, mainly of figures and portraits which are transformed and distorted by the ideas that Bacon found in his own subconscious.◄ Bacon tried to tap into the hidden thoughts and feelings in his subconscious.◄ Bacon's images usually involve huge carcasses and figures placed inside bare interiors.◄

A good example of Bacon's approach is his painting 1946. Bacon's approach was to paint from observation and then let the subconscious mind take over.◄ The huge open carcasses in the background seem to form a kind of crucifixion and suggests that it is passing judgement on the semi-abstract figure under the umbrella.◄ Even Bacon's use of the paint, which is very loose and rapid, suggests violent movement in the picture.◄ The use of colour is very dramatic. The strong reds in the background make the dark, threatening figure stand out even more.◄

Bacon also painted Three Studies for Figures at the Base of a Crucifixion in 1944. The painting shows three Furies, which are violent creatures from Greek mythology. According to mythology, their role was to avenge violations of natural order.◄ Each of the Furies is painted in a bright orange room with a low ceiling and no windows which, I think, increases the intensity of the painting.◄ Each Fury seems to be missing a sense representing blindness and ignorance. To me, the painting represents the loss of all hope.◄ There is also brutality in the way Bacon shows the open snarling jaws and fleshy stumps, representing the unconscious fears and inner terror that Bacon had.◄ Bacon was a very influential artist who showed very unusual ways of expressing emotion in his work.◄

The Belgian artist Rene Magritte was one of the leading artists of the Surrealist movement., which was concerned with exploring the unconscious mind.◄ Surrealist artists lived through the horrors of the First World War. The idea of horror and destruction influenced them. At the same time they were influenced by scientific and psychological discoveries, particularly the idea of the unconscious mind.◄ This made the early Surrealists experiment with ways of representing the unconscious mind through automated drawing which they thought led directly to the unconscious.◄

Magritte was more interested in strange and unusual settings and juxtaposing otherwise mundane objects.◄ In his work Time Transfixed, a toy train emerges from a fireplace like a ghost. Another unusual juxtaposition is in Threatening Weather where a stormy sky is filled with a white, female torso juxtaposed with a tuba. This gives the work a strange, illogical dream appearance which in my opinion gives a sense of fear of the unknown.◄ In Magritte's painting Lovers, two figures are out against a woodland and sky. Despite the simple setting, the painting makes me think about ideas of love and secrecy and whether love is attainable.◄

I prefer Magritte's work as the realism and imagery appeal to me. Bacon's paintings represent a very raw approach, whereas Magritte's subject matter deals with memory and reflection and not the more brutal and violent approach of Bacon.◄

Francis Bacon and Rene Magritte use different approaches to painting strong emotion and unconscious thoughts and feelings in their work. Both artists liked to juxtapose very different scenes in their work and had different methods of painting. However, both artists were influential for future generations who still continue to use the ideas of Surrealism and the subconscious in their work.

(◄ indicated a point worthy of 1 mark)

Roxy Paine, the SCUMAK (Auto Sculpture Maker) (1998)

Alice Aycock, The Thousand and One Nights in the Mansion of Bliss (1983)

Features of Fantasy and Imagination

Artists draw inspiration from many different sources. The experience of being in and interacting with the world, in particular, can influence the work created. When preparing for your Art and Design Studies exam, there are different sources of inspiration that would be helpful to consider with regards to fantasy and imagination.

The use of **dreams** in works of art is usually linked to the art movement Surrealism, though dreams have influenced many other movements as well. In dreams there are usually contradictions of space and time. Things happen that are often impossible in reality. Many artists have strived to represent the workings of the unconscious mind that we experience during a dreaming state, highlighting the fact that they often feel very real.

The vividness of dreams fascinated Surrealist artists such as Salvador Dali and Rene Magritte. They thought that dreams and other experiences such as hallucination and trance-like states were a direct route to the unconscious mind. The distortions of time and space that are experienced whilst dreaming provided these artists with a new source of inspiration.

Another form of dreaming, the nightmare, gave rise to a different source of inspiration for fantasy and the darker side of the imagination. **Horror** is successful because it draws on fear and the ability to shock and frighten. Throughout history, many artists have created visions of horrific worlds or events inhabited by fantasy creatures. Hieronymous Bosch and Matthaus Grunewald created imaginary visions of hell which depicted grotesque and exaggerated images of horror, death and destruction. The Irish artist Francis Bacon also tried to create the direct sensation of horror by distorting and transforming images drawn from his own fears and insecurity.

Along a different route, revolutions in communication and **technology** during the early part of the twentieth century allowed artists to raid the popular and commercial arts of posters, photography and the cinema as sources for fantasy and imagination. In the 1950s there was a huge expansion in popular magazines. This growth fed pop artists with a whole new area of visual culture to use as a source for compositions.

Some artists used the products of the machine age directly in their work in the form of Ready-Mades (Man Ray, Pablo Picasso). Others, such as Max Ernst, were inspired by the possibility of fantastic combinations of machine parts. Contemporary artists like Alice Aycock and Roxy Paine have also been inspired by technology to produce work that seems to function as a piece of technology as well as art. Aycock uses fantasy sources such as games of chance, astrology, Eastern religions, philosophy and odd theories about electricity's potential for conjuring up ghosts and visions of paradise!

Roxy Paine's fantasy creations look like mechanical inventions or strange contraptions. In Paine's SCUMAK (Auto Sculpture Maker), thermoplastic is alternately heated and cooled to achieve a specific height. It is then formed into blob-like shapes that automatically move down a conveyer belt, producing unique sculptures.

Throughout history, **religion**, **myth** and **legend** have also been a rich source of inspiration for fantasy and imagination. In all cases the artist is able to imagine and create an image of something which may not have existed in reality. Sometimes these images are meant to inspire the viewer and remind them of some ideal age or way of living. Other times the creations are purely meant to celebrate religious figures or experiences. Examples of this form of inspiration can be found in every culture throughout the world.

Try this activity with a partner who is also studying fantasy and imagination. In your opinion how well do these works by Moreau, Redon and Ernst communicate fantasy and imagination? How well do they represent the elements of fantasy, myth or religion? Think of sources, approaches and the use of visual elements.

ACTIVITY

TOP LEFT:
Gustave Moreau, Saint George and the Dragon (1889–90)

BOTTOM LEFT:
Max Ernst, The Temptation of Saint Anthony (1945)

FAR RIGHT:
Odilon Redon, Cyclops (1914)

Ives Tanguy, Surrealist Landscape

The whole idea of fantasy **landscape** is common in science fiction movies, computer games and animation, and has been a rich source for the depiction of imaginary worlds in the work of many artists associated with his theme. The nineteenth century British artist John Martin, for example, saw the dramatic and violent forces of fire and storm as the basis for creating fantastic and dramatic visions of nature.

Landscape can also be used to conjure up visions of a more romantic nature to describe imaginary places, idealised worlds or even worlds that may be the product of dreams. The Surrealist artist Yves Tanguy created strange, eerily lit landscapes populated by even stranger, semi-abstract, almost alien forms. No matter what form it takes, the natural environment and landscape around us represent a rich source for the exploration of fantasy and imagination.

Now try this...

Salvador Dali described his work as hand-painted dream photographs. With this in mind, discuss the methods and sources used by Salvador Dali to create this work. Briefly give your interpretation and opinion of the piece.

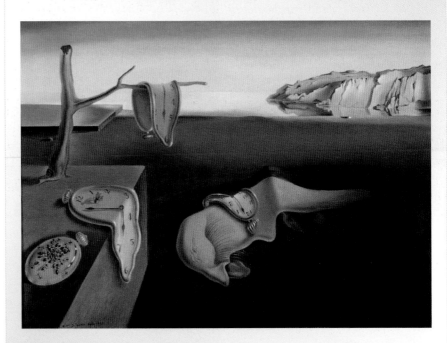

Salvador Dali, The Persistence of Memory (1931)
oil on canvas 24.1x33 cm

Important Movements

ROMANTICISM

In the eighteenth century, artists of all forms began to respond to the Age of Enlightenment. Rather than think scientifically about nature and create realistic portrayals of experiences and existence, Romantic artists such as Caspar David Friedrich sought to explore emotion as a response to nature. Particular emphasis was placed on the emotions of horror, anxiety and wonder, which fit well with the theme of fantasy and imagination.

Henry Fuseli and Francisco Goya are two artists loosely associated with the Romantic Movement in the nineteenth century. Fuseli's *Nightmare* is an excellent example of how terror can be seen in a painting, with the dark horse and goblin lending an ominous presence. Likewise, terror and myth combine in Goya's *The Colossus*. Many art historians claim that the composition is an allegory for the war in Spain. The giant could be seen to represent Spain as a government, or the overwhelming effect of war directly.

Goya, The Colossus (1810–12)
oil on canvas 117 x 104cm

Henry Fuseli, The Nightmare (1781)
oil on canvas 127x102 cm

In your opinion, how well do Fuseli and Goya create a sense of fear in these works? Try to make reference to Fuseli's use of beasts to create the vision of a nightmare and Goya's use of scale. In both cases refer to the way in which colour and shape add to the impact of these works.

Symbolism

The Symbolism movement originated in France in the late nineteenth century and spread across Europe. Their aim was to portray mysterious and odd interpretations of emotions and ideas by using unobvious symbols. These works would often contain grotesque and fantastical imagery such as severed heads, monsters, ghosts and creatures that were part human and part animal. In addition, their works sometimes contained references to the Bible and ancient myths.

Symbolist painting emphasised fantasy and imagination in their depiction of objects. The artists of the movement often used visual metaphors, whereby something is seen to be standing for something else, and symbols to suggest a subject. For the Symbolists art was a means of communicating a personal vision.

Odilon Redon was one of the most important members of this group. In his work he was able to give life to very surreal-like creations long before the Surrealist movement. His works convey a sense of fantasy and dreams and are full of fear and anguish. He was able to communicate very personal visions to create in his art a world beyond that of everyday reality. His strange and uncanny images were important historical links to artists like Chagall and the Surrealists.

Odilon Redon, The Cyclops (1914)
oil on canvas 64x51 cm

Marc Chagall was not connected to the Symbolist movement directly. However, like the Symbolists, he used unusual combinations of symbols in his work. Dreams and memories were powerful sources for his imaginative work. Familiar symbols found in his paintings are winged angels, donkeys, goats, cows, fish, musical instruments and clocks. Changes in scale and unusual juxtapositions of objects all combine with his vibrant use of colour to give a powerful vision.

Marc Chagall, I and the Village (1911)
oil on canvas 192.1x151.4 cm

ACTIVITY

Intermediate 2

Can you find 10 relevant points in this example of a response to a Part A question?

In my opinion Dali uses colour very well to give an impression of a dream-like state in The Persistence of Memory. The light in the picture is very unreal as it is in dreams. He has distorted the watches so that they seem to be melting. In my opinion this is a comment on the passing of time. It appears as if time has stopped and we only have memories of the past left. The strange shape of the creature in the centre of the picture gives me the idea of something being transformed into something else as it happens in dreams.

Dali's painting technique is very meticulous. He uses fine brushstrokes to show every detail. I like the way he paints the still landscape in the background. The strange light and shadows add to the unreal effect in the picture of the insects crawling over the watch and the semi-human features of the creature. It all adds to a sense of mystery and fantasy in the work.

Dali uses familiar approaches of fantasy art such as transformation, distortion and changes of scale to give this work a very unreal effect. In my opinion this is a successful work of fantasy and imagination as it makes you think about the difference between dreams and the real world. Dali must have had a wild imagination to create a work like this. Salvador Dali distorts and transforms the human form into a very realistic nightmare image by changing the setting and placing different objects together in an empty, deserted-looking world of the past.

Surrealism

Of all the areas to study, Surrealism is the most closely associated with fantasy and imagination – partly because of its connection to psychology. It is an important historical movement in art that began in the 1920s and has been associated with artists such as Salvador Dali, Max Ernst, Rene Magritte, Ives Tanguy, Andre Masson and Juan Miro.

Surrealists were interested in the irrational, the spontaneous and the unconscious mind. They intended to show a 'marvellous' world that is beyond the real. The first artists associated with this group lived through the horrors of the First World War which brought death and destruction to Europe on a massive scale, and thought that war was irrational and illogical. Early Surrealists also responded to the changing world of science and discoveries about the workings of the mind, particularly the unconscious.

There have been two main approaches to creating Surrealist images. The first has involved artists trying to find ways of tapping into the unconscious mind. This often means relying on chance effects which come spontaneously. The second approach concentrates more on making paintings that replicate dreams, whereby the image is decided first and painted realistically.

Artists who use the first approach frequently explore trance and dream-like states in order to produce images from the unconscious mind, resulting in what is called *automatic* drawing. By allowing the hand to move across the paper in a random way without control, the artist allows chance to create images that might reflect their subconscious mind. Since the starting point for these works is not deliberately chosen, their meaning can often be ambiguous.

Free-association is an approach taken from psychology. In free-association drawing, the artist draws the first thing that comes to mind in response to an image that came before, without stopping or censoring. Though it may seem random, Sigmund Freud believed that all memories are connected and that through free-association we can access information we didn't know was stored in our minds.

A more deliberate technique used by Surrealists is **frottage**, or taking a rubbing. By placing a piece of paper onto a surface and rubbing a pencil or crayon over it, it is possible to copy the texture of the surface. The resulting image often produces surprising results. Max Ernst was particularly fond of this approach, transferring the grain of his wood floor and the skeletons of fish onto paper and canvas.

ACTIVITY

Frottage, Exquisite Corpses, Photomontage, Collage and Constructed Photography

Try these practical tasks on your own or with a partner. They will help you to understand some of the stranger ideas of the Surrealists and other artists associated with the theme.

Now try this...

Take some rubbings of interesting surfaces, combining them together at random. Look at what you have done and try to use your imagination to find and complete another image from your frottage.

Surrealists have also collaborated in drawing through games such as **Exquisite Corpses**. In this game, each person in a group adds a little to a drawing, folds it over and then passes it on to the next person. Like free-association, the game is intended to unlock the secrets of the unconscious mind.

In a related way, Max Ernst used illustrations from various magazines and catalogues to create **collages**. This approach led to unconnected objects being taken from their usual setting, combined in unusual ways to create unexpected juxtapositions. Calum Colvin is a contemporary artist who uses a method called **constructed photography** to produce three-dimensional images along similar lines. He arranges found objects and materials and then uses paint or computer graphics to combine the assembled objects into a composition.

Now try this...

Take a cardboard box and cut away two sides. Collect different objects and materials and arrange them in interesting and unusual ways. Use your digital camera to photograph the result.

A common feature of Surrealist art is bizarre and inexplicable settings. Although he was not a member of the Surrealists, Giorgio De Chirico was a pioneer of their methods. From 1911–1917 he produced 'metaphysical' paintings. The features of these fantasy works were strange juxtapositions of ordinary objects, hallucinatory lighting and shadows, exaggerated perspective and foreshortening of space. His works are full of the unexpected. He simplified the shapes of objects and used deserted streets and settings from ancient Roman architecture alongside images from the industrial world of the early twentieth century.

Calum Colvin, Mundus Subterraneous I (2007) photograph

De Chirico's favourite objects included trains, towers, ancient sculptures, toys, canons, mannequins, eggs and gloves. In *Song of Love*, a surgeon's glove, a ball and a distant locomotive are set before a shadowy arcade. They all seem unrelated. However, in this metaphysical world new associations are formed. Travel, memories of childhood and perhaps recollections of his home in Italy all feature in his strange melancholy images.

The key to understanding the fantasy element of De Chirico's work is to think of them as visual metaphors and symbols standing for something else. Just as in poetry, the artist uses these to evoke new associations. De Chirico draws us into a world of dreams.

Another artist who used strange juxtapositions and changes in scale was Rene Magritte. Some examples of fantasy in his work are a rock floating like a cloud, an umbrella supporting a glass of water, a pair of boots with real toes and some paintings playing with the idea of light and dark. He deliberately placed objects where they aren't usually found in order to combine two or more contradictory images. Magritte's work is also humorous.

De Chirico, The Song of Love (1914)
oil on canvas 73x59.1 cm

ACTIVITY

Identify the approaches and sources for these works of fantasy and imagination.

Exaggeration, changes in setting and unusual combinations of objects are all approaches used by Surrealist artists to create fantasy and imagination. Discuss how any two of these artists use these approaches in their work. Add comment and opinion on how successful you think they are as examples of fantasy and imagination.

ABOVE RIGHT: *The Song of Love, De Chirico*

LEFT: *Threatening Weather, Rene Magritte*

BELOW RIGHT: *Time Transfixed, Rene Magritte*

Francis Bacon is also a hugely important historical artist whose work can easily be linked to the theme of fantasy an imagination. Bacon painted figures which were frighteningly transformed and distorted by images which he found in his own subconscious mind. This links him to the Surrealist approach of automatism and free-association.

Bacon tried to tap into the primitive forces hidden in the subconscious mind – his works are shocking and can appear very violent, even sadistic. He combined the image of the human figure with religious elements like the crucifixion and painted a series on this violent theme. Common features are huge suspended carcasses, distorted and exaggerated figures set in very sparse interiors, tubular tables and a very vigorous handling of paint.

Ready-Mades, Assemblage and Installation

When preparing for fantasy and imagination you should recognise that the theme is very wide. Though it may be more common to explore the theme in painting, there are plenty of other artists that explore fantasy and imagination in their work.

When the French artist Marcel Duchamp bolted together a bicycle wheel and a stool to make his first Ready-made sculpture in 1913, he established the principle that mass-produced objects could be given the status of art. It was the idea that mattered, not the number of objects in existence.

Ready-mades work on the same principles as symbolism and collage: one thing can stand for another, and art can be created by grouping random objects. In Ready-mades, found objects are juxtaposed and transformed into something else. Marcel Duchamp's *Bottle Rack* and Pablo Picasso's *Glass of Absinthe* (both 1914) pioneered the technique.

Francis Bacon, Painting, 1946 (1946)
oil and tempera on canvas 123x105.5 cm

Now try this...

Try this with any work you associate with fantasy and imagination.

Using the approach of Content, Form, Process and Mood discussed in the Introduction, look closely at the work and analyse it from each of the four standpoints. If possible, discuss your thoughts with a partner.

Marcel Duchamp, Bottle Rack (1914)

Pablo Picasso, Glass of Absinthe (1914)

Assemblage grew out of this idea that just about anything could be used for art. The American artist Robert Rauschenberg used a whole array of combinations and juxtapositions of different objects from the mass media and consumer society of the 1960s. Another American artist, Edward Kienholz, made mini-environments (tableau) from combinations of found objects and casts of people.

> TIP
>
> *Remember to:*
>
> ● *Select at least two artists from different time periods or movements*
>
> ● *Use some biographical knowledge, briefly*
>
> ● *Know the characteristics of your selected artist's work and of the movement they belong to*
>
> ● *Know the approaches used by the artist including the materials, media and methods*
>
> ● *Know the fantasy sources and any other sources of inspiration that they used*
>
> ● *Use the wording of the question to structure your essay into an introduction, middle section and conclusion.*

Exam Preparation

In preparing for your exam you should look in detail at the work of at least **two** different artists or art movements. You should know their background thoroughly, including who may have influenced them. Were they an influence on people who followed on? Were they influential in the development of Fantasy and Imagination? Be sure you can answer these questions thoroughly.

Do not limit your research to a couple of examples from each artist or movement. The better informed you are the more completely you will be able to answer the question paper. Remember that past papers are just a guide to the type of questions that have been asked in previous years. The examiners are always refining the style of question you may be asked. If you have a thorough knowledge of your subject you will be able to respond to changes in questioning.

When looking at work based on the natural environment we should attempt to understand how the artist approached the work and what his main concerns were. Ask yourself questions like the ones that follow to make sure you are fully prepared.

Who made it? Do you know the name of the artist or anything about them? Having previous knowledge about the artist often helps our appreciation of a piece of artwork. This includes knowing what movements the artist may have been involved with.

When was it made? Knowing when the work was made can help our understanding of why it was created. The conditions of the time can have an effect on how the artist approached the task. Technological changes have also, throughout history, had an effect on how artists approach their work.

What is the subject matter? Is the work a realistic record of what was seen? Is the response purely accurate or is there an emotional element to it? Try to identify if the artist is concerned with showing the effects of light on the subject. Determine if the effects of light have been intensified to exaggerate form or space in the work, if the viewpoint is important, and if the objects selected have any underlying meaning. Try to identify what sources, such as dreams or horror, may have influenced the work.

What is the format of the work? What size is it? Decide if it has been made to be viewed in a specific environment. Discover what the work is made from and how the medium has been used. Establish if a particular technique or style of working has been used, and whether it has contributed to the overall effect of the piece.

By answering these questions, as well as those you come up with yourself, you will be preparing yourself to give thorough responses on your exam papers.

Design Studies

Looking at Design

When you look at a work of visual art you might be looking at something that has been created to fulfil no real intended function other than satisfying a need in the artist who created it. Design is different. The designer creates in response to an identified need. He or she is looking to create something which functions for a particular purpose, to be used by identified people in particular circumstances and conditions.

Unlike the visual artist, the designer usually conceives things for other people. They deal with a range of issues and considerations. Each area of design has specific issues that should help you to respond when you evaluate how well a design carries out its intended function.

TIP

Issues and Considerations

Target Market	*Problems*	*Design Issues*
Considerations	*Constraints*	*Consumer Needs*
Aesthetics	*Processes*	*Materials*
Economics	*Ergonomics*	

The graphic designer is concerned with the communication of ideas and information through text, symbols and imagery whilst the architect is concerned with materials and construction methods.

The jeweller will be interested in bringing out the qualities of precious and non-precious materials and using sources of inspiration to create a wearable piece; the product designer is focused on how well a product performs, how safe it is to use and the durability of the materials used to produce it.

No matter what the area of design, it is useful to keep in mind five big questions that you can ask of just about any design:

● Why was it produced? What need does it fulfil?

● How well does it function?

● How is it meant to be used? What is its purpose?

● Who will use it? The target consumer, user, or audience

● Does it look good? What is its style or appearance (aesthetics)?

The chapters is this part of the book will give you detailed advice on approaching each of the six different design areas covered in the Art and Design Studies examination.

2.1

Graphic Design

When we talk about graphic design, what do we mean? In the commercial world, graphic design commonly covers the fields of packaging, advertising, posters, book and magazine design, illustration, newspapers, stamp design, symbols, logos and trademarks, information design and typography. In recent years it also services the expanding Internet in fields such as web design, animation and the design of computer games.

Most students will be involved with the production of either packaging design of some sort, the advertising of a product or service, or illustration. A smaller number may be involved with web design or a related field such as animation. The solution to your brief will likely take the form of a poster, book-jacket, CD or DVD sleeve, labels and/or packaging, point of sale display, stamp design or corporate identity.

The main purpose of graphic design, whatever form it takes, is to communicate with an audience in order to present information. The most important requirement of a graphic designer is a creative mind. The graphic designer needs to be analytical and critical in his or her thinking. Whatever the brief, the designer will need to communicate his ideas in a convincing manner. Most designs will do this using typography, illustration or a mixture of both. If illustration is a part of the design, it may be done directly by hand, using traditional tools such as pencils, inks and paints. It may be conceived and realised entirely on the computer, or it may be a mixture of both, the parts using traditional means being digitally scanned before being manipulated by computer processes. The selection of an appropriate technique is an important aspect of the graphic designer's skills. Most typography design nowadays is achieved using computers.

Example of computer-generated typography

Graphic design as we define it is a relatively recent occurrence. In its earliest form it would have been concerned with the printing of books and pamphlets. Medieval monks produced marvellous examples of illustrated manuscripts, but the process was so time-consuming that the production of a book took years, and only the wealthiest could afford to own any. The book was a precious object, bound in fine leathers and often padlocked to keep it safe. It would mostly be used in churches and monasteries, and would often be read aloud to a listening audience. They were usually bibles or religious texts and were lavishly illustrated. The illustrations were not separate from the text, but integrated into it.

It was really with the founding of universities that secular books came into use. Book production in the twelfth and thirteenth centuries, however, was largely a

In your practical course you will have been concerned with specific design issues. You may have been considering the bold imagery suitable for a poster, or the more subtle effects that may be more appropriate to a book or CD sleeve. Looking at the work of major designers from the period of study will help you become familiar with the approaches others have used when faced with similar problems. This should help you in developing ideas of your own.

A typical Part A question will ask you to comment upon the effectiveness of a piece of graphic design. You will most likely be asked to comment on the imagery, layout, text or colour. You may also be asked to relate it to a particular target audience, or compare it to examples from a different period.

Candidates are asked to comment on the effectiveness of the poster design below. They should refer to imagery, layout and use of colour, and discuss how it may differ from modern designs.

An art nouveau poster

The poster differs from modern designs because it is a lot more detailed.◄ It is from the Art Nouveau period so is very elaborate and stylised.◄ I think this poster is very effective at encouraging people to travel to the area because it shows the beach in the background which is very welcoming.◄ Also I think the inclusion of the woman might encourage some men to go to the area. She is very pretty but not in a way that would be threatening to other women, she looks kind of glamorous.◄ The long stalks of the flowers could represent roads to show where you will end up. The flowers also show the beauty of the area.◄ The use of flowers also gives the poster a very romantic look that could encourage couples to go.◄ The birds around the woman's head also give her an angelic look as well as suggesting wildlife to be seen in the area.◄

The colours are all bright and eye catching. The blue colour in the woman's dress makes it look like the sea, making it look welcoming.◄ The elaborate layout and the use of flowers and curves give the poster an elegant look which would encourage wealthy people to visit the area.◄ The poster is very busy whereas posters today are very simple and give a clear message.◄ The woman is also looking up at the name above the poster (title) like it is a heavenly place to go and is very desirable.◄

(◄ indicates a point worthy of 1 mark)

The response covers all of the points asked for in the question. It focuses on the imagery used and most of the conclusions are sensible if a little repetitive. The layout is covered briefly as is the use of colour and comparison with modern posters. The response is worth full marks.

The graphic designer will have been working in a way similar to you. He or she will have received a brief that will have been discussed with the client in order to clarify what is required. They will have researched the problem and produced a range of possible solutions, one of which will have been refined and used. The design arrived at will have used lettering or images or both.

Most examples of graphic design that you will be looking at will be printed matter like a poster, an advertisement or a piece of packaging. You are not expected to have specific knowledge about the printing processes involved. In commenting on the effectiveness of it, you should consider the aspects of the design that would make it successful.

Ask yourself what market you feel it is aimed at. Does that suggest a particular style of lettering or image? Is the lettering used legible (i.e. can you read it)?

This may or may not be important. There are posters from the 1960s where the style of lettering was very difficult to read. These were still successful because the audience liked the overall design so much they were prepared to take the time needed to find out the information contained.

Sometimes the legibility is very important such as on an information poster or handbill. Legal and financial services advertising used to be very formal and 'stiff' in its lettering and layout, aiming to portray an image of respectability and solidity. Circus posters and handbills, on the other hand, tended to be very garish in the colours they used with large, often outlined lettering frequently suggesting movement or action.

How and where the piece of design is to be used will also affect its design. If the design is for a billboard poster, where people are seeing it while passing by, the message needs to be bold, simple and arresting, probably not using much text. If it were a design for an advert in a magazine, the reader would be able to spend a little more time browsing it. They may in fact enjoy reading a passage of text within an advert. It is important to remember that a solution that is appropriate for one context may not work well in another.

Packaging design also presents its own issues. Anonymous containers for white goods or electrical appliances will typically carry a considerable amount of information about the contents. The appearance of the packaging would not necessarily be a factor in our choice of goods.

Now try this...

Examine these two posters, paying particular attention to the lettering used.

Which poster do you think would have been most effective in communicating its message?

Justify your comparison by discussing clarity, image, composition and colour.

Otis Rush (1967)   *Anonymous (1914–18)*

Packaged items, which we would buy in a supermarket, are different. They may be competing for our attention among similar types of products upon the shelves. The designer will therefore be using some graphic effect to attract our attention. It may be size or colour of lettering, style or content of image, or shape of package.

The size of a package will obviously have an influence on its design. A wine label, for instance is a small surface, usually in competition with many others seen closely together. The designer has the problem of suggesting the style of the wine and any other necessary information within a very small area.

Lingenfelder Riesling wine label

Luxury goods such as confectionery, cosmetics and toiletries also compete on style and appearance of packaging. Some items such as chocolates may use a surprisingly narrow range of colours in their packaging. Gold and purple, with its suggestion of wealth and expensiveness, is a popular choice; most mints use green; red or brown is frequently used for dark chocolate.

Toiletries and cosmetics may suggest luxury or freshness or a clinical background. Their styles and colours of packaging are very diverse. Some use expensive metallic or embossed surfaces to appear luxurious, while others may use illustration or plain materials to suggest nostalgia for a time gone by.

Château Latour wine label   *Farrah's chocolate and toffee*

Product packaging

Compare the two examples of packaging shown above.

Discuss the materials used, lettering and overall style of the different packaging.

What market do you think they would be aimed at?

Justify your comments.

Books and CDs that are examined from a close range by the browsing shopper have their own design issues. They will typically want to suggest or inform us of something about the contents. This may be through illustration, photography or text. Because they are seen up close, the style used need not be bold. The shopper will be interested enough to take the time to come to a decision.

What market would each of the book jackets illustrated be aimed at? Why do you think this is so?

What are the differences in the styles used by the different designers?

Which of the two book covers do you think would be most successful in appealing to its market?

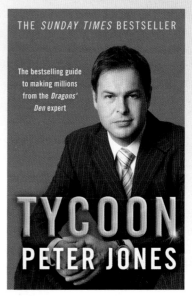

Book jackets have different ways of attracting readers

Magazines are different again. Successful magazines seldom change the layout of their cover once it is established. They often employ some form of 'grid' when designing the layout where the title and information about contents is always in the same place. Different issues are recognisable by a change of illustration or photograph on the cover.

Part B questions will ask you to select designers whose styles differ. You may be asked to comment on how their use of text or illustration differs and to compare the effectiveness of their work. How they achieve visual impact or how they communicate their ideas may also be asked. The question may additionally address marketing or corporate identity, and will ask why they are important.

TIP

When you are analysing a piece of graphic design you have to ask yourself questions such as:

How has the lettering or image used been achieved?

Has it been hand drawn or typeset or is it a photographic or digital image?

Has the designer or illustrator used a particular method or technique?

How does the scale, style or colour of the text affect the design?

If an image is used, is it realistic, semi-abstract or abstract?

Is it imaginative? Does it suggest a scene or theme from a book or film or a mood from a piece of music?

Is it informative? Does it show us how to use or do something, or does it present information in the form of a graph or diagram?

How has the designer used the visual elements of shape, colour, tone, texture or form?

Are they used dramatically to arrest the viewer's attention? If so, has it been done through use of contrast? This may be when the designer wants to compete with other similar images.

Are they used in a limited manner, perhaps to convey mood?

These sorts of questions apply whether the design is hand drawn, photographic or digital.

Example Question and Response

Candidates are asked to compare the methods of visual communication of two graphic designers from different styles or periods. The answer should refer to key aspects of their work in showing why they are regarded as important in their field.

Art Nouveau was most important in the 1890s in Europe and the USA. It was widely used in fashion, architecture and graphic design but was rarely used after the First World War. Although every artist had their own variation of the style, two broad types became apparent. First there was the detailed complex style of artists such as Alphonse Mucha. Then there was the simpler clearer style of artists such as Charles Rennie Mackintosh. It was this second style that later inspired Bauhaus designs.◄

Will Bradley was born in 1868 and he was responsible for introducing Art Nouveau to America through his magazine 'The Chap Book'.◄

Milton Glaser was born in New York in 1929. He was popular in the 1960s and is known for using bright vibrant colours. During his career Glaser has already created over 300 posters.◄

Two posters I will write about are: Victor Bicycles poster by Will Bradley and Dylan by Milton Glaser.◀

Both of these posters communicate their ideas well but use very different techniques to do so. Victor Bicycles by Bradley shows two women riding bikes past flowers. Dylan by Glaser was a record cover and shows a silhouette of Bob Dylan.◀ *Bradley has a very intricate yet simplified style whereas Glaser has a relaxed simple style. The image in Bradley's poster is typical art Nouveau as it contains simplified elongated motifs of flowers. The women are silhouettes but their faces are shown. Their dress and their posture give the poster a very formal style.*◀ *The image of Dylan in Glaser's poster seems hunched over and is very simple, giving it a relaxed style.*◀ *The lettering Bradley uses is very thin and has serifs which also looks formal — and there is also quite a lot of writing making the poster very detailed. In sharp contrast, Glaser used thick lettering which has been forced into rectangles.*◀ *This technique is similar to the 'Beggarstaff Brothers' as their designs were always asymmetrical with heavy lettering to balance the heavy image.*◀ *Bradley seems to be drawing attention to the image so the image will be noticed first because the writing is so thin. Glaser's poster seems more united so everything is seen at once.*◀ *Both posters use the contrast between black and white to make the images stand out but also to make the colours of the posters stand out more.*◀ *Glaser uses a lot more colours in the subject's hair whereas Bradley uses the colours as background to the image behind the flowers.*◀ *Glaser is obviously influenced by the Art Nouveau style because he too uses little tone, bright colours and very few straight lines. A common feature of Art Nouveau is the whiplash line that is used in Dylan's hair.*◀ *Bradley uses the contrast between straight and curved lines to great effect as it makes the curves of the bicycle wheels and flowers stand out.*◀ *Bradley uses the image to advertise bicycles to women and get across the message that they are not just for men. Also using formal clothing styles tells that they are suitable for upper class people and so make the product desirable.*◀ *Glaser communicates the idea of fun through his use of bright colours making the product desirable to young people and making it eye-catching.*◀

Bradley is an important designer because he introduced the concepts of the style of Art Nouveau to many people, making it very popular. Glaser is important because his development of Art nouveau techniques caused them to become iconic in the 1960s and 1970s 'hippy' era.◀

(◀ indicates a point worthy of 1 mark)

Since Art Nouveau is the link between the examples of the designers work chosen, it is appropriate to give a short description of the movement at the beginning. Some of the characteristics of the movement may have been described here. A brief biographical comment is also appropriate. The writer describes the importance of each designer, using examples of their work that illustrate the points he wishes to make. Throughout the answer, he tries to draw comparisons between different aspects of each designer's work — composition, lettering, and colour. Some of the points could have been made more clearly, and there is a little repetition, but overall the comparisons and contrasts are valid.

From the range of possible questions, we can see that a narrow study of one or two individuals will not prepare you well for the exam. You should think about all aspects of graphic design and perhaps tie them in to a couple of distinct periods or styles. This would allow you to answer most comparative questions with some confidence. Remember that many graphic designers work as part of a team, so be sure to find out about other individuals who may be involved in specific periods and styles.

WHAT ARE THE MOST COMMON ASPECTS OF GRAPHIC DESIGN STUDIED IN SCHOOLS?

Poster design must be one of the most popular choices. It is helpful to think about what we mean by a poster. Commonly a poster is printed in some numbers and will be used as a form of advertising a product, service or event. Sometimes posters have no direct commercial purpose, but are works of art in their own right. They have been about since the invention of printing and were initially used to inform the public about civic matters rather than advertise commercially. Their development followed the progress of printing.

As has been said earlier, lithography with its ability to produce large colourful images saw the explosion of poster design. This coincided with the development of mass production methods in industry. New products were produced and the poster became the most effective method of announcing them to the world. Their commercial purpose, advertising the products of the growing manufacturing industries, meant that early posters were wordy, with little in the way of illustration. They had a basic commercial purpose, to pass on certain information, and they mostly stuck to that.

Typesetting machines used in the newspaper industry were developed in the 1880s and 1890s. These machines allowed the typesetter to use a keyboard to set the type rather than set it by hand. The machine manufacturers therefore limited the style of typefaces used in the industry. Poster designers, however, continued to produce hand lettering or set the type by hand; new display typefaces such as Century and Franklin Gothic were developed for their use.

Jules Chéret was a major influence on changing the way posters were designed. In his lifetime he produced more than 1000 poster designs. Due to this, he is sometimes referred to as the father of the modern poster. Chéret was a lithographer by trade and had been influenced by artists such as Fragonard from the Rococo movement. His main output was theatrical posters in which he made the illustration the most important part of the design. One of his great skills as a designer was in combining lettering with an image. Usually the lettering in his posters was done free-hand.

Chéret was able to skilfully combine large amounts of text with colourful exciting images without the lettering overpowering the drawn image. His work is largely romantic in nature, showing stylised figures, usually in action, with the minimum of text necessary to advertise the event concerned. His posters often show lively confident young women with an independent view of the world. Chéret's style was so fresh and popular that it quickly spread from France throughout the Western world.

Others who adopted a similar style included Toulouse-Lautrec and Pierre Bonnard. Toulouse-Lautrec was heavily influenced by Chéret and developed his techniques and ideas further. He fully utilised lithography's ability to print large areas of unbroken colour and treated the poster as a work of art. Like Chéret, he was heavily influenced by the Japanese prints that were becoming popular in Europe at the time and used compositional devices found in these prints in his own work.

Now try this...

Discuss the ways in which colour, image and lettering have been used in creating this poster. How effective is it in your opinion?

Graphic designers need to be able to communicate clearly with their audiences. Compare examples of graphic design from two designers or design groups from different times. Explain how they are effective communicators.

Toulouse-Lautrec, Ambassadeurs: Aristide Bruant dans son cabaret (1892)

The Art Nouveau movement that followed had its own prominent poster designers. One of the most famous was Alphonse Mucha. Although at first glance Mucha's posters are similar to Chéret's in that they both use attractive women to advertise products, Chéret's women have an innocence about them that separates them from the more sophisticated women shown by Mucha. Mucha's work also tends to have many more of the design aspects we would associate with Art Nouveau, such as Celtic symbols and sinuous lines. In Mucha's posters line is used much more to outline forms and separate them from other parts of the design. Other prominent designers who worked in the Art Nouveau style were Aubrey Beardsley, Gustav Klimt, Jan Toorop and Charles Rennie Mackintosh.

Many British designers produced excellent poster designs in the early 1900s. Apart from Mackintosh and Beardsley others such as Dudley Hardy and The Beggarstaffs (Sir William Nicholson and James Pryde) were highly influential. In Britain most of their posters were not considered works of art, as much poster design was viewed throughout the rest of Europe. Instead it was produced solely for advertising cultural events, transport, utilities and products.

In the 1920s, London Transport, under the direction of Frank Pick, commissioned prominent artists of the day to design many of its posters. Their designs usually included Edward Johnston's typeface used by the London Underground. In 1915, Pick first employed Edward McKnight Kauffer, at that time relatively unknown, to design his first poster for the London Transport.

McKnight Kauffer was to go on to become one of Britain's most famous poster designers of all time. Many of the artists employed by Pick were established painters and consequently the images used on London Transport posters echoed the artistic styles of the time. There were posters commissioned that were heavily influenced by Cubism, Futurism and Vorticism. The quality of London Transport posters was so high that in the 1920s and 1930s designing one for the organisation was regarded as a significant artistic achievement.

Alphonse Mucha, Job cigarette papers (1894)

The Beggarstaffs (1897)

Edward McKnight Kauffer,
London Transport poster (1974)

As the world began to climb from the economic depression of the 1930s, large organisations such as Shell, the GPO and the BBC, following the lead of London Underground, became influential in promoting good graphic design in Britain. These organisations employed leading artists and designers such as Rex Whistler, Edward Bawden and Eric Ravilious in the production of their advertising and publicity materials.

Now try this...

How successful do you think the book jacket illustrated here would be in attracting its audience? Refer to imagery, typography and layout in your response.

Compare the work of two graphic designers from different times or movements who have achieved visual impact in their designs. Describe their methods of doing so.

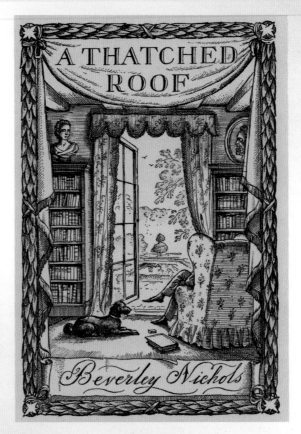

Rex Whistler, book jacket

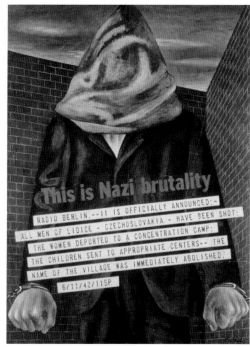

RIGHT:

Fix-Masseau, Pierre Felix, The Life of the Railway (1929) colour lithograph

FAR RIGHT:

Ben Shahn, This is Nazi Brutality (1942)

In Germany in the 1920s and 1930s new ideas about typography alongside photography were being used, such as in Bauhaus-influenced designs, whereas in France traditional methods of poster design flourished. Drawn images were to remain the dominant style. Cassandre was one of the most famous and influential French poster artists.

During the 1930s and 1940s film became an important method of mass communication. It was used for entertainment, recording news events and as a means of propaganda in the Second World War. Film reporting the progress of the war was shown in cinemas on the same programme as the main film. Newsreel reporting was to become a feature of a cinema visit up until the time TVs were available in every home.

As printing presses and ink technology developed, photographs in newspapers became more prominent and magazines, such as *Life*, which were largely composed of photographic reporting, had a large following.

Poster design, however, remained a very important method of persuasion. In wartime, posters were used to recruit personnel for the forces and to educate the public. There was an expansion in the range of information posters aimed at aiding the war effort. Fougasse (a pseudonym of Cyril Kenneth Bird) and Abram Games, who had previously worked for Shell and the Post Office, were to become two of the most influential British poster designers of the war period. In America, Ben Shahn and Norman Rockwell were among a group of artists and illustrators who worked for the Office of War Information.

In the 1950s the influence of America, as seen in films and TV, grew throughout the world. With growing prosperity new markets expanded and the advertising of products and services became a growth industry in its own right. TV became the foremost broadcasting medium and commercial advertising was supplied by the advertising agencies of the day. New York was the centre of the advertising industry where the biggest firms were located. The main products were cars,

Saul Bass, Film Poster (1959)

household appliances, food and tobacco products. They were advertised widely on TV and adverts for them took up many pages of the popular magazines of the day.

The 1950s also saw the start of the arms race with political positions strongly supported on each side. Information design became an expanding field as governments and newspapers explained their views and positions. Information graphics was seen as an effective means of transmitting complex statistics.

Among the most prominent American designers of the period was Paul Rand who specialised in corporate identity, Saul Bass who was an important film and TV graphic designer and Robert Brownjohn who worked in both New York in the 1950s and London in the 1960s. Brownjohn was famous for his typography, film titles and album covers for the Rolling Stones.

The teenage market of the 1950s was a new phenomenon and designers catering for it developed new styles of graphic design. Record covers and cosmetics became more important in a competitive, expanding market where rock 'n roll imagery had a wide appeal. Posters featuring their stars advertised films of the day, as the studios resisted the increasing influence of TV. The use of TV advertising was seen to be the most effective means of reaching an audience. As advertisers switched from print to television and advertising revenue decreased, weekly magazines struggled and eventually ceased to be produced. *Picture Post,* a magazine that pioneered photojournalism, ceased production in 1957.

Due to its position within the communist bloc, Poland did not have a competitive commercial market. Its graphic designers, who had been internationally appreciated since the 1930s, now mostly produced book illustrations and cultural posters for such things as the circus, theatre and the active Polish film industry. Designers such as Henryk Tomaszewski and Roman Cieslewicz were a great influence on art students in the West.

The 1960s saw New York cease to be the world centre for the graphics industry. American topical magazines had had a global influence on graphic design until then. The increased availability of colour TV bringing its own style of graphics, faster communications via satellite links, and up to the minute news caused the famous magazines such as *The Saturday Evening Post, Look* and *Life* to close down.

Throughout the 1960s there was a major repackaging of the corporate identities of many of America's biggest companies. Designers such as Eliot Noyes, Paul Rand, Saul Bass, Milton Glaser and others changed the outward appearance of many international corporations through logos, signs, packaging and transport.

At the same time in Britain, commercial television was growing and requiring graphic design that kept up with the times, both in its programme titles and adverts. British industry also looked to modernise its public appearance with new corporate identities for the railways and British Gas, amongst others. The publishing and newspaper industries in Britain were also changing. Developing technology and colour printing in newspaper supplements brought new freedom to designers, while publishers such as Penguin established new 'house' styles.

Paul Rand, Logos

Increasing prosperity throughout the 1960s saw re-branding being carried out across Europe. Graphic design was almost an international obsession. The 1964 and 1968 Olympic Games saw international co-operation in developing unique signage and typefaces for each event. The influence of pop and psychedelic culture was apparent in the production of record covers and 'underground' magazines. Designers such as Peter Max and Wes Wilson produced some of the most memorable graphic design of the period.

In the 1970s the introduction and development of computer-aided design in the graphics industry created new styles and layout. Tasks that previously would have been impossible, or required great technical skill, were easily achieved using a computer. Information and corporate design flourished in Britain with a greater public awareness of 'brands' being established.

Punk, with its anti-establishment message and style, was another major influence. The 'street' style of Punk was to influence the 1980s magazine styles. Both *The Face* and *i-D* were very influential in their style and layout that at times appeared 'mock amateur'. Terry Jones and Neville Brody were the most influential designers of the time.

Computer-aided design was to explode in the 1980s and 1990s. It is an easy medium with which to produce collaged and layered images; both suitable for the increase in information technology. Company reports were no longer printed as dull tables of statistics, but were designed with interesting graphic inserts to cater for an expanding share-owning population.

Photomontage and photography were also widely used and rigid 'grid' typography loosened up as the computer easily allowed paths of lettering and blocks of text to be set at angles. The ordered systems of the past were less influential as individuality became a major objective of designers.

None of this would have happened without the progress that had been made in printing technology. Offset printing became the norm and colour was no longer a luxury, allowing for full-colour images to be quickly and accurately produced.

Despite the ease with which computers can manipulate images, many designers do not use them for their initial brainstorming and creation of ideas. This is because the choices available when using the computer can hinder creativity in different ways. The designer can be restricted by the range of typefaces and mark-making available in the computer's programmes, as none of the options available may be the most suitable to communicate the message he or she is trying to put across. New ideas can also often come from exploring different media and techniques. Hand-drawn ideas are not at the mercy of a computer programme and can therefore be more quickly developed in the initial stages of designing when ideas are developing rapidly. Additionally, the rapidity with which the computer can change images can also hinder the creative designer. Too many choices can lead to indecisiveness.

Exam Preparation

In preparing for your exam you should look in detail at the work of at least **two** different designers or design movements. You should know their background thoroughly, who influenced them, and whether they were an influence on people who followed on. Find out if they were influential in the development of graphic design.

Do not limit your research to a couple of examples from each designer or movement. The better informed you are the more completely you will be able to answer the question paper. Remember that past papers are just a guide to the type of questions that have been asked in previous years. The examiners are always refining the style of question you may be asked. If you have a thorough knowledge of your subject you will be able to respond to changes in questioning.

When looking at graphic design we should attempt to understand how the designer approached the work and what his main concerns were. Ask yourself questions like the ones below to ensure that you are fully prepared.

Who made it? Do you know the name of the designer or anything about them? Previous knowledge often helps our appreciation or a piece of design.

When was it made? Knowing when a design was made can help our understanding of why it was created. The conditions of the time can have an effect on how the designer approached the task. Technological changes have also, throughout history, had an affect on how designers approached their work.

What is the purpose of the design? What message is it trying to get across to the public? Is it meant to package, sell, inform, or educate? Is it aimed at a particular audience or market? Is it designed to last some time, or is it temporary?

What is the format of the design? What size is it – is it small scale like a book, or large like a hoarding? Is the work a 2-D design? Find out how the original was made i.e. photographically, freehand. If it is a package or other 3-D design, discover what materials it is made from. Are these materials recyclable or otherwise environmentally sound?

Look closely at how the typography is arranged, whether it is integrated with the image or separate. What is its overall impact: is it calm or exciting? How do the visual elements of line, colour, form, pattern etc. contribute to the design?

Research where the piece is meant to be viewed: inside or out, in good light or in dull lighting conditions? Do you think it is successful in fulfilling its purpose? And, finally: Do you like it?

By answering these questions, as well as those you come up with yourself, you will be preparing to give thorough responses on your exam papers.

2.2

Product Design

Product Design is usually about functioning objects that are produced in quantity through mass production. They are those designed objects that perform a specific function such as clocks, lamps, mobile phones, televisions etc.

If you have done product design in your practical work for the course you will already be aware of the need to address design issues. In your design unit, you will have worked to the specifications and constraints of the design brief and hopefully solved the problem that you set out for yourself.

When you evaluate your design, try to estimate how well it meets the specifications that were set out in your original brief, within the constraints and the design issues identified. Thinking about your own work as a designer is very good preparation for thinking about the examples of product design that you will face in the Art and Design Studies exam.

Part A Questions

The range of products that you might be given in Product Design can come from just about anything that is designed to meet a human need within the last 260 years. Product Design questions are usually about designs for everyday objects that perform specific functions in our lives. These objects are typically mass-produced and involve industrial processes. Answering the question can be quite straightforward when you think of the design issues related to this kind of design.

> **TIP**
>
> *Always remember the 5 big questions about design*
>
> *Why was it produced and what need does it fulfil?*
>
> *How well does it function?*
>
> *How is it meant to be used? What is its fitness for purpose?*
>
> *Who will use it? Who is the target consumer, user or audience?*
>
> *Does it look good? What is its style or appearance?*

WHY WAS IT PRODUCED AND WHAT NEED DOES IT FULFIL?

It is important to know why a product was designed. In some cases you need to consider *when* it was designed as this can influence how it looks. In product design the designer needs to establish exactly what the user wants. Along with a client they will agree to a brief just as you do in your practical work. A detailed design specification will follow after considerable research into what is already out there in the marketplace. This will cover key design features like function, safety, materials, ergonomics and aesthetics. In the real world of product design and development, production processes and costs will be important factors.

HOW WELL DOES IT FUNCTION?

Function is a hugely important design issue in Product Design. What it does and how well it does its job will be crucial to products like cars and cameras, for example. Things aren't much good if they don't work!

You may be asked to judge the effectiveness of a product compared with similar ones. To function well a product must serve its purpose, as well as be safe for the user. In exam questions you are asked to speculate on the safety of a product for its intended user.

Now try this...

Think of these four products.

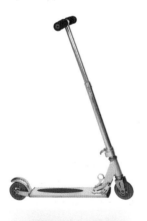

TOP LEFT:

portable scooter

TOP RIGHT:

Victorinox Rescue Tool

BOTTOM LEFT:

Juicy Salif Lemon Squeezer

BOTTOM RIGHT:

Morphy Richards kettle

What safety features did the designers of these products have to consider?

How is it meant to be used? What is its fitness for purpose?

It is important to choose the right materials for the product. You need to consider what the product is made from, how it is made and how suitable the materials are. This is becoming increasingly important as we have to be efficient with natural resources and careful with the environment.

If the product is intended for hard wear and tear then it must be durable. Often, you have to consider the properties of the materials used in the manufacture of a product and what they can and cannot do. Are the materials appropriate to the style? Are the materials appropriate to the function?

Ergonomics is the study of humans in relation to their environment; how we relate to products when we are lifting them, holding them, wearing them and so on. To be fit for purpose a product must be able to be handled well. Its moving parts must be of appropriate shape. If it is a computer, for example, you must be able to see the controls.

When thinking about a product design, you should think about how easy it would be to use. If it is easy, comfortable or efficient it will generally be fit for purpose and, as a result, make our lives easier. You will already have experience of some similar products that are easier to use than others. Think of mobile phones, MP3 players and games consoles. Terms like user-friendliness and user-interface are used to refer to how easily and trouble free a product is to use.

Another factor which helps to make a product useable is Anthropometrics. This is the science of human measurement. It is about how well the product relates to the size and scale of the human body. Making something too big or too small will make the product difficult to use and it will, again, be unfit for purpose.

Both ergonomics and anthropometrics ensure that products are comfortable and easy to use. Designers use anthropometrics to work out the correct proportions for their products.

Who will use it? Who is the target consumer, user or audience?

The target market or demographic group are the consumers for whom the product was designed. It may be a particular age group, social group or ethnic group. It is important to identify the users of a product to show whether the product meets their needs and if it is fit for purpose.

There is a constant demand for new and improved products. Sometimes demand is driven by the desire or pull of the consumer. Sometimes it is a new development in technology, materials or manufacture that creates the opportunity for a new product. Just think of the changes to popular consumables for young people like the mobile phone, the computer, the iPod, games consoles and cars and you will see that products are always changing in response to shifts in culture and consumer demand.

There is competition in the market place and product designers are always targeting products. New technologies and media are powerful forces, constantly pushing the designer to create new products and whetting the appetite of the consumer for the latest design. The iPod is a very good example of this just as the Sony Walkman was when it was first launched in 1979. However, new does not always mean good.

As a consumer yourself, you can ask yourself how one product compares to a similar one. In the examination, you may be asked to judge the effectiveness of a product from the past compared with similar ones that you use today. This should only happen with examples that have been in common use for some time, like a television or car. Do not assume that because something is new it is better. Analyse each example to find its positive and negative aspects.

In your opinion what gives these two products popular appeal to the target users?

SwiMP3 by Finis, underwater MP3 player

The original 'Walkman' model TCS 300 made by Sony of Japan

Think of function materials, fitness for purpose and aesthetics.

TIP

The electronics company Sony led the development of transistors to replace big valves in radios so that they could be made much smaller.

German Designer Dieter Rams was head of design with the consumer electronics manufacturer Braun. Having worked with the company for over forty years, he became a very influential industrial designer. Rams' work has been called 'elegant and supremely versatile' by critics, including those with the Design Museum. For Rams, there are ten principles that every 'good design' must meet:

- Good design is innovative.

- Good design makes a product useful.

- Good design is aesthetic.

- Good design helps us to understand a product.

- Good design is unobtrusive.

- Good design is honest.

- Good design is durable.

- Good design is consequent to the last detail.

- Good design is concerned with the environment.

- Good design is as little design as possible.

(Source: www.designmuseum.org/design/dieter-rams)

ACTIVITY

Take a few examples of Product Design that you have studied and discuss them in a group using Dieter Rams ten principles for good design. Have each member of the group make a case for the best-designed product.

ACTIVITY

ABOVE LEFT:

Malcolm Park Vacuum Cleaner

ABOVE RIGHT:

Dyson Vacuum Cleaner

BOTTOM LEFT:

Lambretta LD 150 scooter 1957

BOTTOM RIGHT:

Aruliden SCOOT

Compare the modern and older examples of the vacuum cleaner and the scooter.

In your opinion how do they compare?

Think of function, technology and aesthetics.

DOES IT LOOK GOOD? WHAT IS ITS STYLE OR APPEARANCE?

Styling is about a product's visual appearance. Most products that we use in our homes and offices work well enough, but styling helps to give the product consumer appeal. It is what helps to set a product apart from its competitors. An important aspect of style is Aesthetics: a set of principles of good taste and the appreciation of beauty.

Just as with painting and sculpture, some products can be very easily identified as belonging to a particular style. The sleek lines and style of the Malcolm Park vacuum cleaner of the 1930s, for example, remind you of the Art Deco Movement.

The form and shape of a product influences its style, and styles can differ hugely among similar products. Some products, like mobile phones, perform the same basic function but are styled differently as market trends, materials and technology change over time. The form and shape of products contribute to their appeal as well as their ease of use.

ACTIVITY

 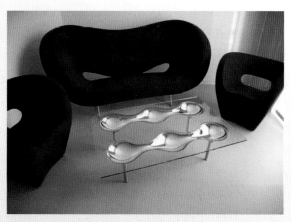 

Marc Newson, Felt Chair   *Ron Arad, Sofa & Chair*   *LC Tiffany, Mosaic Dragonfly Table Lamp*

The appearance and feel of a piece of design make it appealing and influence the user's choice in a competing market. Style, aesthetics and appeal help to sell the product. Our lives would be very dull if everything looked the same.

In your opinion, which design features of these products make them appealing to users? Think of form, style and function.

ACTIVITY

How would you rate the style, aesthetics and appeal of this common product?

Icona Kettle by De'Longhi

Questions

The first thing to do with a product design question is to sort out the design issues identified.

Evaluate the success of this product in terms of form and function. Compare Starck design with the form and function of other kitchen utensils you have used?

or

What is your opinion of this product? How fit for purpose do you think it is? Refer to materials, function and style and similar products you have used.

Juicy Salif Lemon Squeezer, Philippe Starck

This question asks you to compare the product with ones that you use. Perhaps a lemon squeezer is not used too much in your house. Still, you can easily see that Philippe Starck thinks that well-designed objects must do more than perform with ergonomic efficiency. Starck believes that objects have the power to make the most boring tasks fun.

If you see the appeal of the product being about a wide range of benefits to the user you will be given credit. The obvious fun element in Starck's design and the insect-like quality of the squeezer as being part of its appeal would gain marks for you.

Its function is to squeeze the juice from a lemon into a user-supplied container. The flutes or channels squeeze the juice and direct it downwards to the point and concentrates the juice where it drips into a glass. The space between the legs is where the glass is put to collect the juice, so you might argue that Juicy Salif performs its function well. If the absence of a supplied container to collect the juice is a negative about it, then you might argue that it is not fully fit for purpose.

You might consider the ergonomics of the design to be an important factor in its fitness for purpose. The shape at the top is designed to take a half lemon so it can be pressed downward using the palm of the hand. So the Juicy Salif seems to fit well around the main contact or user interface – the palm of the hand. The rise at the top of the leg is to ensure that the juice does not run down the leg. The tripod legs are there to provide stable support, but would this be the case on a slippery surface?

Now try this...

How many of these words can you apply to the Juicy Salif?

Expensive, durable, futuristic, happy desirable, fashionable, flashy, friendly, fun, functional, intelligent, novel, smooth, streamlined, space age, trendy, high tech, elegant, modern, classic ...

Look at the Juicy Salif again. Think of all the design issues involved. How well does this answer deal with the question?

The lemon squeezer is very streamlined and modern and trendy.◄ Its function allows the lemon to be hand pressed and turned on the top of the ribbed pointed squeezer.◄ This directs the juice down the ridges to a centre point where they collect and drip down straight into a container which the user must add.◄

The legs of the squeezer are long, thin and elegant like the legs of a giant insect, they point upwards to stop the juice from dribbling down.◄ They are widely spaced out to provide stability.◄ The material is stainless steel which is very durable, not too expensive and easily cleaned.◄ However, the user may have difficulty fitting the container beneath the squeezer and it may slip around depending on the force used by the user.◄

The shape of the squeezer suggests that it is for show and not for use around children as the pointed legs could be dangerous.◄

In my opinion more effort has been placed on the appearance of the squeezer than on function. The curving main body, oval shape and sleek appearance are all aesthetically pleasing.◄ The emphasis has been on making it look distorted and space age a theme that was popular in the 1980s and 1990s.◄

Compared to other kitchen utensils its form is unusual and quirky. Normally kitchen utensils are made safe for frequent use with rounded edges and non-slip bases.◄

Despite this the squeezer has great appeal for the modern user and would fit in with the fashion conscious idea of having a designer kitchen.◄ It would also be fun to use and to look at compared to the common plastic lemons squeezer with the circular base and ridged plastic peak which are easy and safe to use.◄

(◄ indicates a point worthy of 1 mark)

This response really tackles the issues in the question and would achieve full marks at Higher.

Discuss the strengths and weaknesses of this multifunctional toolkit design. Why do you think it is still a successful product today?

or

In your opinion how do the functions of this product contribute to its lasting appeal?

At first sight you might think it difficult to sort out the design issues identified in both questions. Like the scooter question, they ask you to consider the good and bad points. The questions also hint at the fact this product has been around for a while. It has stood the test of time resulting in lasting appeal since the original design by Karl and Victoria Elsener over a hundred years ago.

The good points seem to outweigh the bad points but listing them will help:

Good points	Bad points
Many different functions	Safety
Portability	Social factors
Durability	Danger
Form	
Appearance	
Compactness	
Practical	
Engineering	
Materials	
Ergonomic	
Cost effective	

Now try this...

Think of the design issues involved in a Swiss Army Knife. Consider the good points and bad points and the structure of the question. Now read this and identify as many relevant good and bad points as you can.

The Swiss Army Knife has much strength. It is very compact and versatile. It has many useful tools but is still small enough to fit into a pocket. The combination of plastic and stainless steel for the different tools makes it very sturdy.

The form of the knife is well shaped for the human hand making it ergonomic and providing a secure handle for using any of the tools inside. The tools fold away securely into their sockets in the body of the knife so there is no danger of them becoming loose and presenting a hazard to the user.

Another strength is the use of bright colours like red and yellow. The tool is used by campers so it is easily found if dropped.

The strengths of the knife definitely outweigh the weaknesses, otherwise it would not have remained a popular tool for so long. However, the user might have difficulty pulling out the tools from the body as they are they so small. Disabled users might find this even more difficult. Also the tools are not as effective as their full-size versions.

I think it is still a very successful product today as it has adapted to the demands of different generations of users by adding things like tweezers, a toothpick and a corkscrew.

In your opinion how well does this shopping trolley meet the needs of the users? Consider function, materials, ergonomics and safety.

Compare it to the shopping trolleys that you see in supermarkets.

Shopping Cart by Ideo (1999)

TIP

The international design consultancy IDEO like to begin the design process with a thorough process of market research. For the concept shopping cart, they considered not only user needs but checkout operators and trolley collectors. They photographed and filmed users at every stage of their use of the trolley and how people carried their shopping away.

Think of all the advantages that this shopping trolley would bring to the user. Supermarket trolleys always seem difficult to manoeuvre through the aisles. Would the back-wheel steering solve this problem?

Very often, supermarket trolleys are just one large basket on wheels that do not allow the shopper to organise the shopping. Would this trolley allow the user to store goods easier using the spaces provided for plastic baskets? How do the other features, such as hooks for hanging carrier bags, a slot for holding a cup of coffee and another for transporting flowers, affect the trolley's use?

In terms of safety, do common supermarket trolleys consider child safety? This one incorporates a secure child seat which also has a play tray.

Supermarket trolleys need to be lightweight so they can be pushed easily through aisles. Does this trolley use materials better than the average trolley? How so?

Consider how the designers of this trolley identified the user's needs and incorporated them into their design.

Laptop computer

Porsche Cayenne GTS

Western Electric Dial Telephone

Fruit-friendly lunch box by Concentrate

Part B Questions

Whether at work, travelling, in the home or at play we are surrounded by objects which play a significant role in our daily lives. In the period covered by this course mass-produced consumer products have affected the quality of our lives and environment. One look at the products opposite and you can see what we now take for granted in our daily lives.

Your practical work can help you with the design issues that you need to analyse in Part A questions. These design issues are the same in Part B questions. In the latter you are being asked to show your knowledge and understanding of designers, design, groups, movements, periods and/or styles that you have studied for the course.

A typical Part B question will ask you to select two important product designers from different periods or styles. Your choice should be designers who have changed design in some way or developed new approaches which have influenced the way we think about design (e.g. Bauhaus or specific designers such as Marcel Bruer, Dieter Rams or Jonathan Ives). It helps if you choose identifiable designers that the marker is likely to know. Choosing unknown designers or obscure examples may make it difficult for the marker to form a picture of the products you are writing about. As with other areas of design it is an advantage to be able to show the main characteristics of any design movement that you choose. In other chapters on design in this book you will find lots of information about the evolution of styles like Arts and Crafts, Art Nouveau and Bauhaus.

The Part B question requires you to combine your historical knowledge with your ability to analyse and evaluate the success of a product along the lines of the five big questions discussed earlier. You should practise using the five big questions to analyse designs as well as researching the individual designers you have chosen to study in the course. When you study any movement or period concerned with product design, you should build your knowledge of the style, influences, technological changes, manufacturing and materials associated with the period. This includes exploring the origins of product design as well as the daily life of individuals at a specific time.

The origins of what we now call product design are to be found in the development of industrialisation and mechanisation in Britain around the late eighteenth century. During the two hundred years that followed, this development continued with the introduction of new materials and processes, leading to the design of the products and appliances that we know today.

In addition to the introduction of pioneering materials, the Industrial Revolution also created a new demand for products. Changes in lifestyle led to fresh and rapidly expanding markets. An excellent example of this is the design of domestic ceramic products. The demand for pottery had been increasing in the eighteenth century due to population growth and, among other things, the popularity of drinking tea.

To meet the growing demand for his popular ceramic tableware, Joseph Wedgwood devised a method of multiple reproduction using pre-cast moulds, patterns and mechanical lathes to speed up the production of what in the past had been done by one individual craftsman. Innovation was a key factor in the success of his work as he continuously sought to improve on the pottery techniques involved in the production of ceramics. During the late 1750s he developed a new and brilliant green glaze which could be used to decorate moulded earthenware items in the form of fruits and vegetables.

Wedgwood demonstrated that mechanisation need not lead to poor quality in design. He was able to virtually mass produce functional, economical domestic objects for a specific target market without compromising aesthetic appeal.

By the mid nineteenth century, increased mechanisation allowed for the production of standardised parts for a range of products. The development of the factory production line enabled the process of manufacture to be broken down into stages and products assembled from these standardised parts. Increasingly, designers turned to machines to speed up production and to exploit new possibilities for the style of objects created by machines. High precision cutting tools such as lathes and power tools began to be integrated into the production lines of factories.

Michael Thonet (1796-1871) used machine-formed rods of wood bent under steam pressure to produce his very functional and practical bentwood chairs. Bentwood chairs required no jointing and were easy to assemble using screws. The flowing elegant and simple design of these chairs ensured their popularity so much that they are still produced today.

ACTIVITY

Choose two product designers working in different periods or styles. Discuss how their ideas have contributed to the way we lead our lives. Refer to specific examples of their work in your answer. Why are they important?

TIP

Use well-known important historical or contemporary designers. In this way you can be sure that the marker will recognise who you are discussing.

Thonet's success was due to his ability to use mechanised methods of construction economically. While not all product designers took to mass-production techniques, many used it to help develop user-friendly, functional items that changed the way people lived and worked. This also led to the ability to create different products with similar designs, and construct brand images.

In the last two hundred years, product design has been influenced by many movements that use different routes to production. From the hand-crafted, individual pieces of Arts and Crafts and Art Nouveau to the streamlined, machine-aesthetic of Bauhaus and Modernism as a whole, product design has undergone many transformations. In the twenty-first century product designers face a world of global warming, population growth and dwindling resources. Designers are now looking for sustainable design solutions using materials which are environmentally friendly. Today, there is a greater emphasis on economic, environmental, ethical and social issues in product design which is likely to drive designers to seek new solutions to the form and function of the products used in everyday life.

Exam Preparation

In preparing for your exam you should look in detail at the work of at least **two** different product designers. The designers you choose should have had an obvious impact on the development of product design and you should be able to discuss them in the context of design movements, historical context etc.

Do not limit your research to a couple of examples from each designer or movement. The better informed you are the more completely you will be able to answer the question paper. Remember that past papers are just a guide to the type of questions that have been asked in previous years. The examiners are always refining the style of question you may be asked. If you have a thorough knowledge of your subject you will be able to respond to changes in questioning. Ask yourself questions like the ones below to ensure that you are fully prepared.

Who designed it? Do you know the name of the designer or anything about them? Previous knowledge often helps our appreciation or a piece of design.

When was it designed? Knowing when a design was made can help our understanding of why it was created. Previous knowledge often helps our appreciation of a piece of design.

What is the purpose of the design? What is its function target market etc.? Is the product itself new, or is this a new design to reinvent or compete with an established product?

How well does it look? Does the product have visual impact? Does it look good? What is your opinion of it?

Does it function well? How well does the product do what it is supposed to do? Has it been made with appropriate materials? Key issues such as safety and ergonomics should also be considered here.

By answering these questions, as well as those you come up with yourself, you will be preparing to give thorough responses on your exam papers.

2.3

2.3 Interior Design

Interior Design is about designing spaces that suit the needs of the people who will use them. The designer is therefore concerned with structure and layout, decoration and style and all the colour fabrics, furniture and fittings that go into making a fully functional space suited to its intended purpose. The range covered in the course could include domestic interiors, places of entertainment, transport, public spaces, shopping and places of work.

From the start of your course you should try to look at a range of different interiors old and new. Most big department stores like IKEA, John Lewis and Habitat have displays of their latest domestic and office interior designs. Museums, like Kelvingrove Art Gallery in Glasgow and the National Museum of Scotland in Edinburgh, have displays of interiors of the past. Seeing things in the round is always better than simply studying photographs.

A typical Part A question for both Higher and Intermediate 2 may ask you to write about any designed interior within the period of the course. It will ask you to identify the specific interior design issues of the space facing the designer or give you the choice of some of them to discuss or comment on.

The question may ask you to identify the design features that make it a successful interior. It is therefore worthwhile making yourself familiar with the kinds of design issues facing the interior designer. Many of these are similar to those of product and architectural design, so you should therefore look at those chapters to give you a full picture of design issues. Here are some additional elements to consider:

WHY WAS IT PRODUCED AND WHAT NEED DOES IT FULFIL?

All designers set out to solve a particular problem. It may be a need or gap in the market or to make an existing space look or perform better. Whatever the example, you should try to think about why the interior was created.

HOW WELL DOES IT FUNCTION?

Function is about how well a space works as it was intended (i.e. a dining room or office). When you think about function, consider what it was designed to do. Functionality is an important aspect of interior design because if the different functional elements of the space do not work the look and feel of the space will be affected.

Barajas Airport terminal Madrid

Corridor of Mackintosh Building, The Glasgow School of Art

Always remember the five big questions about design:

Why was it produced and what need does it fulfil?

How well does it function?

How is it meant to be used? What is its purpose?

Who will use it? Who is the target consumer, user or audience?

Does it look good? What is its style or appearance?

Joe Colombo, *Habitat of the Future*

When you consider how well an interior is functioning, remember to give your opinion. How easy is it to get around the space? How many different activities can, and are meant to, be performed in the space? If it is a car interior, how accessible are the different controls for the driver?

Take into account safety issues in your analysis. Is the design practical and comfortable? Would it be accessible to individuals with different physical challenges? Make sure you note any aspects of the design that do not function well. Asking these types of questions will also give you an opportunity to write about ergonomics and anthropometrics. Ask yourself how well the designer understands and responds to human dimensions and movements and how well they fit into the interior.

Finally, give thought to the materials used in the design. How well have they been used? Do the different materials used (i.e. fabrics, textures) work well with one another?

EXAMPLE

Use the five big questions to evaluate how well this kitchen design would meet the requirements for this kind of interior.

Are the materials natural or man-made? Are they suited to the interior and its intended use?

Walls and floors are large areas of an interior making it important to get the right look and feel. You should look at surface finishes and if they help to create the illusion of space and size.

Just as in product design, there are other aspects that have consumer pull. Interior designers are very conscious of fashions and taste and will use style and appearance to appeal to particular users.

Gullwing Oak Kitchen

How is it meant to be used?

You should assess how well the interior does what it is supposed to do. Consider if it is meant to be used differently than spaces that serve the same purpose (i.e. formal dining room compared with family dining room). In most cases you can compare interiors to things you have already seen since each of us experience interiors every day. Think of kitchens, sitting rooms and your school. You can score highly here at both Higher and Intermediate 2 by giving good reasons for your answer. Is there any aspect that is not fit for purpose?

ACTIVITY   Intermediate 2

In your opinion how well does this interior space meet the needs of the user? Refer to layout, function and use of materials.

Porsche 911 Turbo interior

Who will use it?

Just as with product design, think about the target users of the interior space. Who will use it? How well has the interior been designed to meet their needs? This is important because some interiors have to function specifically for certain types of users.

You should already have an idea about what the needs of users are from the interiors that you have studied. Ask yourself if there is any aspect that does not meet the user requirements. Consider the variety of people and abilities that exist and decide who would or would not benefit from using the space.

Does it look good?

There are many factors that contribute to the appearance of an interior. This question has to do with style and aesthetics. The aesthetical quality of an interior space will be affected by the choice of furnishings, how they are arranged and the colours and textures used.

The Salon, Glasgow

Discussion of furnishings and fittings are really important in answering interior design questions. You shouldn't attempt to analyse these simply as individual products though. What is important is how the furniture and fittings contribute to the overall effect of the interior. This influences the functionality and fitness for purpose of the interior as a whole. Good layout also contributes to the ease of use of the interior; achieving a balance of all the different furniture and fittings is essential.

Considering such things as fabrics and decoration allow you to evaluate the impact of visual elements on the mood or atmosphere created by various colour combinations, patterns and textures and their contribution to the appearance of the interior. At all times you can use these as reasons to explain why an interior functions well and/or helps to make it appealing or user-friendly to the intended users.

The overall style of the interior can be crucial to how well it looks and feels to the user. If you are studying Higher then an historical knowledge of movements such as Art Nouveau, Post-Modernism and High Tech can help you recognise particular styles. Interior designers try to create certain effects with their combinations. They set out to create harmony, unity, variety and contrast. Contrast can be introduced through different shapes, heights and sizes as well as texture and lighting.

A designer might use colour, texture, light and pattern to create effect. He or she might use rhythm by repeating features such as regular spacing of lighting, seating and desks or tables. To create emphasis, the designer will make some elements more important than others for effect and impact and to give a focal point to particular parts of the interior.

Balance also contributes to the appearance of a well-designed interior space. Balance can be achieved through symmetry and asymmetry; be formal or dignified. Asymmetry involves achieving balance using different weighting, sizes and scale. Having an awareness of scale and proportion means that things should not look out of place and that all the parts of the space relate well to each other.

Finally, designers must consider how people might react to an interior. We use language such as lively, depressing, functional, and so on to describe the overall expression of the space. By thinking about your immediate responses to an interior and finding language to describe it, you can state strong opinions to include in your exam answers and back them up with solid reasons.

Part B Questions

As with other areas of design it is useful to have a broad overview of the knowledge and historical context of Interior Design. If you combine this with a good knowledge of evaluating interior design along the lines of the five big questions you should be well prepared. When you understand what the theme is about, you can add depth to your study by further research on the individual designers and movements mentioned in the overview. It is a good idea to focus your preparation on at least two historically important areas or designers clearly identified with interior design. However, a wider knowledge of interior design and the ideas associated with it will also help you with your study.

OVERVIEW OF INTERIOR DESIGN

The Industrial Revolution in the second half of the eighteenth century was an important landmark in the emergence of interior design. The development of manufacturing industries and the growth of large cities in Britain changed the way of life for people in the nineteenth century. Previously, the home had been the place of work as well as comfort, living, eating and sleeping. As the place of work began to be removed to factories, offices and shops, the home began to acquire a distinctive character.

As a result, new ideas about how the interiors of home, entertainment, travel and leisure should look began to emerge. Items of household decoration such as wallpaper, textiles, carpets and furniture began to be mass-produced using new industrial methods. The new middle classes who began to inhabit the suburbs of the growing cities were keen to use these products to create comfortable interiors with lots of ornaments, pictures and surface decoration to show off their new found wealth. The fashion was for colourful, soft and plush interiors. Professional interior decorators began to emerge and important architects integrated interior design with the total design for their buildings.

In the second half of nineteenth century, the idea of interior design was new to many people. Existing styles tended to copy things from the past. A whole industry had grown up around replicas of past styles (Classical, Gothic, Medieval). These were popular choices for the interiors of public buildings, for example: The Houses of Parliament, churches, schools, Glasgow University and railway stations such as St Pancras in London.

The great exhibition of 1851 at Crystal Palace in London had been an important landmark in design. Many new factory goods were on display. The reaction to this for a lot of designers at the time was that hand-made traditional goods were the best. Truth to materials meant that the natural state of the materials should not be altered.

William Morris was the founder of the Arts and Crafts Movement. Morris believed that there should be an artistic presence in the interior design of a house. He detested mass-production and believed that good interior design could only be produced by working creatively with natural simple materials.

The Red House at Bexleyheath built around 1860 illustrates Morris's approach. The interior of the house was left to Morris and his friends to design. Morris' dislike of the interior design of the day was obvious. He could find nothing that

> **TIP**
>
> It is a good idea to have some contextual knowledge to use in your essay.

> **TIP**
>
> In Higher Part B questions on Interior Design you must show knowledge and understanding of two different interior design styles, designers or movements. At Intermediate 2, you need to know two different designers, interiors or two different styles. It is a good idea to choose well-known, historically important designs or designers. They are recognised as the most important and influential.
>
> It can be an advantage to use these designers and movements because you can get lots of historical and contextual information about them. Choosing unknown designers may leave you struggling for important knowledge and understanding of their significance and their influences.

RIGHT: The Red House (1860)

he could use in the house so everything was designed from scratch. He believed in using simple construction showing the natural quality of the materials.

Morris and his friends went on to form a company aimed at bringing Arts and Crafts ideas about honesty and truth to materials using traditional craftsmanship to the wider public. Morris & Co. was one of the earliest interior design firms. They produced carpets weavings, wallpaper, hand-printed fabrics and furniture such as the Sussex Chair. Made from natural turned ebony wood the chair was simple, practical and elegant at the same time.

Morris & Co. had a huge influence on interior design taste. However, by the 1920s the firm had declined. New companies influenced by Morris & Co. such as Liberty and Heals were producing items for interior design at more affordable prices. The rise of modern machine-age technology was to bring back mass-production with an emphasis on quality design.

EXAMPLE

The Arts and Crafts movement began in England during the late nineteenth century. Influenced by Gothic and medieval art and craft, these artists and designers rejected the emerging mass-production techniques in favour of hand craftsmanship and the use of natural materials. They wanted to make design suitable for everyone. Arts and Crafts designers achieved most of their aims except design for all because their designs were so expensive to produce.

In my essay, I am going to compare Arts and Crafts interior design with the Bauhaus. Bauhaus, which means built house, started in Germany in 1919. This school of thought believed in using machine technology in designs. Function was important, but they also believed that everyone had the right to good design. They used simple shapes to make fashionable objects.

An introduction such as this will score you several marks.

ART NOUVEAU

Art Nouveau is another very popular choice for questions in this area of design. It spread across Europe and into America in the 1890s and is easily identified with wavy, flowing forms based on sinuous line and ornament derived from natural shapes. Art Nouveau is also known for the repeated use of dynamic whiplash line to unify the appearance of interiors. This was a very extreme form of styling and may be considered exaggerated and contorted. These stylistic features became typical of Art Nouveau interiors and were used on plasterwork, doors, windows, furniture and light fittings.

As Art Nouveau became an international style of interior design in the late nineteenth and early twentieth century each important designer contributed a very unique interpretation of the style. The Belgian architect and designer Victor Horta was one of the first to develop this style. His Hotel Solvay of 1895 shows all the richness of Art Nouveau when applied to interiors. All the furniture and fittings were made to Horta's own designs and specification. The flowing whiplash lines combined with motifs from art are present in almost all aspects of the interior.

Antonio Gaudi designed complete interiors with very organic and flowing shapes. His approach took the contortion and exaggeration of Art Nouveau form a stage further. Casa Battlo and Casa Mila are both apartment blocks designed by Gaudi in Barcelona in the early years of the twentieth century.

Gaudi basically invented his own language of design. The irregular-shaped interiors of Battlo and Mila have lava like forms and waving ceilings, strangely curved windows and door frames. Furniture designed by Gaudi himself was also wildly exaggerated with fantastic curving and twisting forms reminiscent of bony and wiry structures. For Gaudi, a building and its interior should grow around only a rough plan, leaving the rest to creative inspiration.

ART DECO

When a question asks you to discuss the influences on designers or their sources of inspiration you should be able to describe some of the main characteristics of a style. Art Deco is a very distinctive style in interior design that could be useful to you in your responses.

Gaudi, Casa Battlo

In the 1920s when Art Deco developed as a style, Modernist designers were beginning to emphasise function, technology and industrial processes in the design of interiors. Art Deco, on the other hand, was a luxurious style which drew on a wide range of very exotic influences and sources. Designers used materials such as zebrawood, ivory, tortoiseshell and leather to add variety to interiors. The features of the style are easy to recognise. Sharply angled forms, zigzag shapes and rich geometric patterns along with motifs derived from tribal and ancient Egyptian art give Art Deco interiors a very distinctive appearance.

By the 1930s, Art Deco had spread widely in Europe and America. In America, designers were attracted to the streamlining which had begun to appear in products such as cars. The range of motifs started to include the star and sunburst along with influences from Hollywood film sets. Art Deco interiors

Frank Lloyd Wright, Robie House

Charles Rennie Mackintosh, Mackintosh Room at The Glasgow School of Art

combined sharp edges with smooth surfaces and contour lines. Designers adopted the sleek lines and metallic finishes of industrial products, trying to reflect the modern idea of speed and dynamic lifestyles.

The architects and designers Frank Lloyd Wright and Louis Sullivan helped to spread this style to America. Like the European designers, Wright wanted to design inside and out. His career spanned several periods of design, with a range of public, private and commercial interiors.

His Prairie Houses are very good examples to use in an essay. They are called this both because they were near the great expanses of land stretching beyond Wright's home in Chicago, and because the low, horizontal profile of the homes resemble the flat prairie spreading out across the Great Plains. The Robie House (1909) is a very good example of this flowing integrated design favoured by Wright. The form of the interior is based on interlocking verticals and horizontals. The focus of the design is the central core of the stone fireplace. Wright used natural wood material such as oak to give a unified feel to the interior.

Charles Rennie Mackintosh was perhaps the most original designer/architect working in this period. Famous as the architect of the Glasgow School of Art he was better known for interior design. Mackintosh combined influences from Japanese art as well as the floral designs of his wife Margaret Macdonald with his own designs to create a distinct style that has spread around the world. In Glasgow alone the linear lines and curving florets can easily be seen on window grates and in glass windows throughout the city.

Now try this...

Compare the work of two interior designers from different periods or working in different styles. With reference to examples of their work, explain the differences in their approaches to interior design. Why do you consider them important to the development of interior design?

ACTIVITY

Evaluate the following essay response. Which comments would earn the writer marks? Where is there room for further development?

One of the most important examples of Mackintosh's interior design is the drawing room of his townhouse. In 1906 Mackintosh moved to Southpark Avenue in Glasgow and re-designed the Victorian interior of his new townhouse.

In the drawing room, Mackintosh created a dramatic effect by using pure white for the walls, floor coverings and furniture. This unifies the interior and helps to create a light and airy space for the comfort of the user. The overall design is very rectangular and shows the clear difference between Macintosh's approach and the curves and flowing shapes of Art Nouveau.

Mackintosh developed his furniture designs mainly based on geometric forms. Despite this, you can still see evidence of his use of natural forms in the motifs on the chairs, fireplace and lights. The placing of the furniture gives a balance and helps to unify the interior giving it a unique style.

An analysis like this could easily pick up 4 or 5 marks. You should always include in your exam answers a conclusion which identifies the historical importance of the designer or design. So, why was Mackintosh important?

Mackintosh was never fully happy with Art Nouveau. His influences took in natural form and flowing lines of Art Nouveau but he looked wider, to Japan, the traditional look of Celtic design, the great ancient castles of Scotland and the Arts and Crafts movement. Mackintosh designed from the inside out carefully accounting for the user requirements. He combined style and function in an innovative way. His use of modern methods led to a lasting influence on interior design.

Now try this...

Examine the Library of the Glasgow School of Art to create your own evaluation of an example for the middle section of an essay on the same question.

Introduction

Write a short paragraph with some contextual background on interior design based on the information in this section and your own Art and Design Studies. Write a short paragraph giving some historical and biographical information about CR Mackintosh and why you have selected him as one of your chosen designers.

Middle Section

Choose appropriate design issues given for interior design in Part A questions and use them to evaluate the example of the Library of the Glasgow School of Art.

In Part B questions at both Higher and Intermediate 2 levels you will be awarded marks for some relevant historical and biographical knowledge. However, the real substance of any middle section of an essay will deal specifically with the main features of the designers approach, methods, style and influences. You should support this with relevant examples of their work that you can critically and historically evaluate.

Library, Glasgow School of Art, 1909

Conclusion

Use the information in this section and your own Art and Design Studies to write a short conclusion on the importance of Mackintosh to interior design.

Marcel Bruer, Wassily Chair

Mies Van Der Rohe, Barcelona Chair

MODERNISM

By the first decades of the twentieth century the telephone, electric light and travel by air ship and car had all been achieved. These technological developments widened the scope for interior designers. New sources of power, technologies and industrial process became available. Up to this period, however, approaches to interior design had looked back into time for inspiration. Modernism was the name given to a new form of design that would take on-board all of these developments of the new 'machine age'.

The Schroder house was built in 1924 by the Dutch architect Gerrit Rietveld. Rietveldt belonged to a movement called De Stijl (The Style). Geometric and abstract forms dominate this modern interior. New materials such as steel, concrete and aluminium were used in the construction of the house. Rietveldt used only primary colours throughout the interior to give a sharply defined look. His use of space is different from anything before. It is broken up by different planes to define areas from one another, and the furniture and fittings are designed with stark, simple shapes.

The founder of the Bauhaus School of Design, German architect Walter Gropius, was another designer who responded to the challenge of new materials of the machine age. Gropius believed that all design could be functional as well as aesthetically pleasing and stylish. As a result, Bauhaus interiors were bare and usually painted white. There was no place for the kind of decoration and historical influences that you would find in previous styles. There was no wallpaper, carpeting or patterned decoration, nor was there any room for detailing on doors, woodwork and plasterwork. Bauhaus used materials which suited the new style such as tubular steel, leather, plastics, linoleum and wood. Two examples which show their approach to design of furniture and fittings are the Wassily Chair and the Barcelona Chair.

ACTIVITY

Compare the approaches to the design of furniture for interiors of Mackintosh and the Bauhaus. To get started, think of the ideas behind Art Nouveau and Bauhaus.

Modernism became the dominant style in design among leading designers for a large part of the twentieth century. Yet all of the previous forms of interior design were, and still are, available for consumers to mix and match according to their preferences. Modernism led the way as it contributed major new ideas about the way in which we think about interior spaces. New synthetic materials and fibres, vinyl, melamine, plastic and glass fibres are some of the materials that modernist designers adapted and skilfully incorporated into design.

Depending on your Art and Design Studies coursework there are many European and American designers that you can use to show the importance of modernism in interior design.

ACTIVITY

Compare the work of two interior designers (such as Rietveld and Horta) from different periods or working in different styles (like De Stijl and Art Nouveau). What influenced their ideas about interior design? Why do you consider them important to the development of interior design?

Gerrit Rietveld, Schroder House

TIP

- *Rietveld was influenced by abstraction, geometry, art and new materials. Horta was influenced by natural and organic forms.*
- *Rietveld was one of the first modernist designers. Horta used influences from the past.*
- *Rietveld's work influenced the Bauhaus.*
- *Art Nouveau was one of the first movements to move interior design away from the historical styles of the past.*

POST-MODERNISM

Dissatisfaction with the limitations of modernism had been stirring in the design world from the 1970s when, in 1981, a group of mainly Italian designers formed an anti-modernist design group called Memphis (after a song by Bob Dylan). Unlike modernist design, it is hard to describe function in Memphis design as they were so against modernist doctrine. They had an experimental approach to design using very unconventional materials and took influences from just about all historical periods, including art movements such as Pop Art, Cubism and Surrealism. They were attracted to materials such as printed glass, celluloids, neon tubes and zinc-plated sheet-metals jazzed up with flamboyant colours and patterns, spangles and glitter.

Victor Horta, Hotel Solvay

Basically, Memphis threw out the notions of good, functional design and began to incorporate thought-provoking ideas about how interiors should look. They tried to transform influences from popular culture into classy, surprising and quirky design. Memphis designers, including Ettore Sottsass and Michael Graves, laid the foundations for a new approach to design.

Running alongside this development, some designers were trying to use functionalism in a new way. High Tech interiors allow for the display of service functions such as ducting, wiring and piping in a decorative way. The Pompidou Centre in Paris is an example of one such structure. Rather than hide the air ducts and other building facilities within the walls, the designers chose to exhibit them as an attraction as interesting as the modern art displayed within the building.

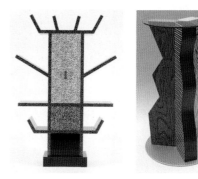

Ettore Sottsass designs

Post-modern designers turned away from the functional and minimal use of materials and ornament in modernist design. 'Form follows function' was one of the rules of modernism which really meant that how something looks should come from what it is supposed to do. This was too restrictive for Post-modern designers who wanted to show that form was as important a feature in design as function.

Pompidou Centre, Paris

Many Post-modernist designers have used a combination of past, present and future in their designs. By combining the old and new together in different ways, designers are able to create experiences and environments that might not have otherwise existed. Such designs are at times entertaining and odd, humorous and baffling. The results are often unexpected and quirky: odd angles, unconventional material usage and creative style integration. Though many Post-modern designers seek to create spaces that are comforting and calming, there is often an air of excitement and, sometimes, social commentary involved.

We now live in a world where ideas about interior design are shaped by so many different influences it is no longer possible to think of designers belonging to any one movement. In the twenty-first century we are more concerned with the environment and sustainability than ever before. The Internet, mobile phone technology and faster, more powerful computer-aided design allow ideas to spread very quickly. The whole history of interior design styles and materials is instantly available to the designer, no matter where they are in the world.

As a result some contemporary designers do not fit easily into any category. Phillip Starck's interiors often include unconventional materials with lots of surprise elements. He combines straight lines with flowing curves in his designs for furniture and fittings; designs single products and undertakes large-scale interior design projects for hotels and public buildings.

Philip Starck interior

Frank Gehry is another designer who does not belong to any fixed style or approach. As an architect, Gehry distorts forms and makes them collide into each other in almost random fashion. You will see structures together at very odd angles in Gehry's work. This approach allows for some very unusual internal spaces. Gehry's work will be discussed in more detail in the chapter on Architecture and Environmental Design.

Exam Preparation

In preparing for your exam you should look in detail at the work of at least **two** different designers or design movements. You should know their background thoroughly, who influenced them, and whether they were an influence on people who followed on. Find out if they were influential in the development of interior design.

Do not limit your research to a couple of examples from each designer or movement. The better informed you are the more completely you will be able to answer the question paper. Remember that past papers are just a guide to the type of questions that have been asked in previous years. The examiners are always refining the style of question you may be asked. If you have a thorough knowledge of your subject you will be able to respond to changes in questioning.

When looking at interior design we should attempt to understand how the designer approached the work and what their main concerns were. Ask yourself questions like the ones below to ensure that you are fully prepared.

Who made it? Do you know the name of the designer or anything about them? Previous knowledge often helps our appreciation or a piece of design.

When was it created? Knowing when a design was created can help our understanding of why it was created. The conditions of the time can have an effect on how the designer approached the task. Technological changes have also, throughout history, had an affect on how designers approached their work.

What is the purpose of the design? What message is it trying to get across to the user? What is its function? Is it aimed at a particular audience or market? Is it designed to last some time, or is it temporary?

Who is meant to use the space? What size is it? How is the space laid out? What materials are used and how do they work together? Are these materials recyclable or otherwise environmentally sound? Research how the piece is meant to be used: what are its aesthetical qualities and how functional is it? Do you think it is successful in fulfilling its purpose? And, finally: Do you like it?

By answering these questions, as well as those you come up with yourself, you will be preparing to give thorough responses on your exam papers.

2.4

Architecture and Environmental Design

CR Mackintosh,
Glasgow School of Art (1897–1909)

Richard Rogers, Barajas Terminal,
Madrid Airport (2006)

Like interior design, architecture and environmental design is something we interact with all of the time. It surrounds us everywhere we go. Our homes, businesses, schools – all the spaces we live in – have been purposefully designed to serve different purposes, and with specific functions in mind.

As in other areas, there are issues specific to architecture and environmental design. In the Art and Design Studies examination you may be given several views of a building including a close-up to help you examine the key features being asked about in a Part A question. You will be asked to write about an example of architecture from any time in the last 260 years. This period covers huge changes in styles and the construction methods used by architects.

The example given may be a public building, domestic architecture or a piece of environmental design. It may include things like public spaces, play areas and street design such as bus shelters. You can practice for questions on architecture and environmental design simply by taking a walk and looking at the structures around you. Remember that every time you enter a building you will be a user. This means that exploring the areas around you should include considering how the structures were designed to be used and how they are used in reality.

A bus shelter is a common piece of environmental design which can be adapted to numerous different urban environments. What design issues need to be addressed in this shelter?

How does such a design benefit the user?

Use your mobile phone camera to record buildings and examples of environmental design that interest you. Produce an electronic sketchbook with notes on features that you think are interesting.

Evaluating Architecture and Environmental Design

All Part A questions at Higher and Intermediate 2 will ask for your opinion. Your opinion should be based on reasons which you can justify. Always remember that the architect has worked with clients to establish a specification for the building. Knowledge of the considerations that have to be thought through and the kind of problems that the architect solves in the design brief will help you to justify the reasons you give for any opinion that you express.

So, what question should you ask about a piece of architecture or environmental design? Here are a few of the specific design issues around which you can form your opinions on the success of any example of architecture. They will help you to look closely and evaluate the range of examples in the examination. Of course the more general design issues that you have learned about in your course work apply to architecture as well. These will really focus your responses on key issues affecting architecture and environmental design.

SITE

The site of any building or structure is important. It provides different opportunities for the architect to shape the structure to the site, as well as imposing restrictions. A gap street space in an inner city site, for example, poses restrictions on the width of a structure. An area of land near a wetland or river presents other considerations.

There may also be existing surrounding features to be taken into account that will influence the architect. The new structure may have to fit in with the existing line of a street. It may have to be made from similar materials and be of a similar height and mass to an adjacent structure or it may stand-alone and be deliberately contrasting with existing structures.

Science Centre and BBC Waterfront

141

LEFT: Frank Lloyd Wright, Falling Water (1934–37)

RIGHT: Richard Rogers, Lloyds Building (1979–84)

If the site is in the countryside, the building may have to be in keeping with existing features and be sensitive to views of the landscape. It may have to be horizontally or vertically emphasised so that it fits in with the landscape and surroundings. Good examples of this are the famous Falling Water by Frank Lloyd Wright and the Lloyds Building by Richard Rogers.

What did both Wright and Rogers have to think about when considering the site for the two buildings?

Norman Foster, Hong Kong and Shanghai Bank (1979–1986)

FORM

Form is all about the basic three-dimensional visual elements of the structure. Asking questions about a building's line, shape, texture, colour composition and tone can help you to respond to an unseen example of architectural design.

A really good architect will combine the visual elements with the structural requirements. If you look closely at this famous contemporary building you will see that the structure is supported on the outside using a combination of ladder-like masts and coat hanger beams or trusses. Services, like the lifts and ventilation shafts, are all on the outside of the structure. The architects carefully considered the visual appearance together with the form to create a stunning piece of architecture.

If you think of the structure as an object you can consider whether it is a cube, cylinder, sphere, cone or a composite of all of these. It may be a linked series of forms: cylinders, octagons, cubes etc. Thinking of basic forms when you analyse architecture is important.

You should be prepared to identify very different approaches to the use of form when approaching your exam. Frank Gehry is renowned for his abstract sculptural use of it – a good example to look at is the Guggenheim Museum in Bilbao, Spain.

The forms of the Guggenheim seem to defy all previous ideas of architecture. Using computer-aided design techniques, Gehry was able to shape unique forms which are irregular and asymmetrical. They seem to merge into each other and clash at the same time. Nonetheless, Gehry has succeeded in creating huge volumes of form which, clad in a shining metal surface, immediately grasp the attention of the visitor to the Museum.

Now try this...

Look again at the illustrations of The Shanghai Bank and the Guggenheim Museum.

How well do both architects use visual elements to give these buildings a strong visual appearance?

Frank Gehry, The Guggenheim Museum Bilbao, Spain (1997)

SCALE

Scale is about the comparative size of the different forms in the structure. Architecture is scaled to meet the requirements of the site, the appearance and the various functions needed. It can be used to emphasise specific features and to give a sense of importance to a building. Tall skyscrapers such as the Chrysler Building in New York achieve this by using strong vertical lines to emphasise its soaring height.

Gothic architects used spires and towers to create scale. Large civic buildings such as The Houses of Parliament in London use scale to suggest importance. Such architecture is often described as monumental or grand in scale. The success of many buildings is a result of the careful consideration of scale in relation to the site and location of the building. A building can look out of place if it does not fit the existing scale of its surroundings.

FUNCTION

The purpose of a structure is important and asking questions about its function will help you to consider how well it performs its service. What is the building used for and who is going to use it? Does it meet the user's needs? Asking these questions about the building allows you to write about safety, comfort and other things that make the building fit for its purpose.

Think about the different activities that go on in different types of buildings. If it is built to provide recreation, like a cinema, theatre or concert hall, the architect will need to provide comfort, safety and good views of the performance area. If the building is used for religious purposes, the design should allow for a focus on the most sacred and symbolic areas. Similarly, office spaces have specific functional requirements to allow the user to access equipment and communications. Even the most basic dwelling house needs to function well to provide for human needs like eating and sleeping.

CIRCULATION

Architecture is about creating spaces for people to do different things. When considering circulation, you'll want to think about how people access the building and how they move throughout it. In many examples you will be able to consider factors such as rooms, offices, storage, corridors and entrances to help you assess the circulation and comment on how well space has been used.

Basic considerations like heating, ventilation, fire escapes, elevators and lighting all have to be designed by the architect. In the Lloyds and Shanghai banks the various functions of the building were deliberately designed on the outside of the building.

In the Lloyds bank, Richard Rogers designed the piping for services such as water, waste and heating to run on the exterior of the building. This makes them accessible for maintenance. Importantly, it also allows the architect to use the shapes and forms of these services to create a stunning visual impact. By freeing up the internal space for other purposes, the design offers better circulation throughout the interior.

Giving consideration to the problems of circulation can also explain the form of the building. From the outside, the Hong Kong and Shanghai Bank does not give much away about the vast open space created by the atrium inside.

Norman Foster, Atrium of the Shanghai and Hong Kong Bank

APPEARANCE

Asking the question 'How well does the structure look?' leads to questions about style and aesthetics. Some simple descriptions are useful to start with such as Traditional, High Tech, Mechanical, Modern and Post-modern.

Consider whether the building has special architectural features. The structure may have an identified style such as Art Nouveau, Art Deco or Bauhaus. These styles are popular areas of study for the course because they are clearly defined styles and examples are abundant.

How do the architects Charles Rennie Macintosh and Antonio Gaudi use visual elements to create impact in these two examples of their work?

Art Nouveau detail of Casa Battlo

Art Nouveau detail of The Glasgow School of Art

Try to point out aspects of appearance created by the use of visual elements such as line, colour, shape, pattern and texture. Architects will often use these to create emphasis or impact. The windows of the Casa Battlo and the entrance to The Glasgow School of Art are very good examples of this.

Some knowledge of architectural styles will help when considering appearance. It is possible that you might even experience a piece of contemporary architecture like the Chiat/Day building.

Frank Gehry worked with the Pop artist Claes Oldenburg on this design. They were using a model while trying to decide how to treat the entrance to the building when Oldenburg placed his binoculars in the model. Everyone liked the effect, so it was incorporated into the design. Humour and dramatic effect can be key parts of the architect's design considerations.

Frank Gehry, Chiat/Day Building, Venice, California (1991)

The images below left show one of the most well-known examples of Scottish architecture, The Glasgow School of Art by the famous architect Charles Rennie Mackintosh.

What are the key features of this architectural design that contribute to its distinctive appearance? Identify what you think the architect's primary design considerations would have been in relation to the function of this building. Give reasons to support your answer.

The question asks to identify key features of the building and then go on to explain how the architect has used other aspects he would have to consider for the function of the building.

Note down the main design features you are looking for and find examples in the building.

Design Feature	Example
Siting	street site, north-facing facade
Form	balcony railings, sweeping entrance
Scale	huge windows to let in strong light for art students to work, two floors, follows the street line
Function	specially built for artists
Circulation	sweeping access steps from the street level to an elevated ground floor
Appearance	style of Art Nouveau combined with Scottish baronial style
Materials	sandstone, glass and iron, traditional materials

In response to a question like this you would write about the huge scale of the windows and extensive use of ironwork on the balcony, weather vanes, windows and railings, the stonework, the sweeping curves and interlocking forms contributing to its appearance. If you know more about the Art Nouveau style of Mackintosh, as he is a popular architect to study, you can use some of this to expand your answer.

A typical Part B question will ask you to select two architects or environmental designers from different historical periods or who work in highly contrasting styles. The question will then ask you to discuss, compare or contrast examples of their work. You will be required to discuss characteristics of their work and explain why they are important figures in the world of architecture or environmental design.

Like other areas of design, the period 1750 to the present day saw immense changes of styles, materials and methods of construction in architecture. You clearly cannot study the whole history of architecture, but you can make yourself aware of the more prominent styles. In this period there were several revivals of older styles, new styles and rapid development of materials and construction methods, therefore some selection will be necessary.

The Influences of the Past

Important architecture is long lasting and can influence generation after generation of architectural styles and methods. Without some understanding of the influences of the past it will not be possible to understand the importance of the Neoclassical, Gothic Revival and Arts and Crafts movements of the nineteenth century.

It may seem odd to start your study of architecture by looking at fragments and ruins, but you may be surprised to learn that the architects of ancient Egypt, Classical Greece and the Roman Empire gave us methods of construction, use of form, proportion and structure that survive today.

THE CLASSICAL STYLE

The Classical style of architecture was based on a simple post (the column) and lintel (cross beam) system. The strong emphasis on form and proportion gave Classical architecture a very grand and important status. In most cities and towns in Scotland and abroad you will see the influence of ancient Greek, Roman and even Egyptian architecture. The style had lasting appeal and was used by European and American architects throughout the late eighteenth and nineteenth centuries.

The Parthenon 5th Century BC, Greece

Church on the Hill, Glasgow

National Gallery of Art, London

Town Hall, Paisley

Cumberland Terrace, London

On a very grand scale the architect Robert Adam designed the area to the north of Princes Street in Edinburgh called the New Town. The fronts of the rows that make up the New Town incorporated Classical features such as columns and entablatures. William Playfair, likewise, designed many of the buildings that are crucial to Edinburgh's most famous views such as across the Mound to the Castle and of Calton Hill.

ABOVE:
Entablature of Classical Architecture

FAR RIGHT:
St Vincent's Street Church, Glasgow

TIP

If you live close to any of Scotland's big cities you should look for examples of Classical types of buildings.

Alexander 'Greek' Thomson looked even further into the past. He practiced an almost abstract form of Classicism. He combined Egyptian and Oriental influences to create a unique style in his hometown of Glasgow.

Between 1856 and 1859, Thomson designed the St Vincent Street Church. He made it look like a Greek temple from the front, using decorated motifs from Greek and Egyptian architecture. Unlike some who used this style, Thompson was creative and inventive. He borrowed from the past but interpreted it for his own personal uses.

GOTHIC REVIVAL

For much of the period from 1750 into the nineteenth century, the Classical style was the popular choice with important architects. But in the late eighteenth century, architects in Britain began to look again at another of the great historical styles.

BELOW:
Flying Buttress ceiling

BELOW RIGHT:
Rib Vault ceiling

Just like the Classical style, Gothic style dates from the thirteenth and fourteenth centuries and has never really disappeared. Between 1840 and 1880, the Gothic Revival was an important movement in architecture. Nineteenth century architects revived this style in support of the growth in Romanticism and interest in medieval times.

The main features of this style are the use of pointed and soaring architectural forms. The style is mainly associated with cathedral architecture, but has been used in other structures as well. Pointed arches and towers with decorated

pinnacles are among the most characteristic features. The original Gothic architects tried to create virtual walls of glass so that they could fill the interior with the glow of light through highly decorated stained glass. To build higher and higher they developed the use of the flying buttress to support the thin structure which shaped the interior space.

Gothic methods of construction also included the use of rib vaulting which allowed them to create a new method of roofing. These two methods allowed the architects to create tall interior spaces full of light and space and to give the impression that the cathedrals reached upwards towards heaven.

Two very good examples of the Gothic Revival style are the Houses of Parliament and St Pancras Railway Station designed by AWN Pugin/Sir Charles Barry and George Gilbert Scott, respectively.

ACTIVITY

Select, discuss and compare the work of two historically important architects from different periods or styles.

In your exam you are likely to be asked to refer to such things as style, influences, materials, working methods, form, function and space. As with all Part B questions, you will need to estimate the importance or each element.

The Classical style and the Gothic Revival are highly contrasting styles and were popular in different periods and would be a good choice for comparison.

TIP

If you are writing about styles you should widen your knowledge of historical influences.

During the eighteenth and nineteenth centuries, architects looked to the past for inspiration. The Classical style of ancient Greece and Rome became very popular for stately homes and religious architecture.

In the late eighteenth century, architects began to be interested in Gothic design, which was very different from Classical, and revived the building methods and features of this style. The leading architects were Robert Adam (Classical) and Gilbert Scott (Gothic). Their work clearly shows the differences between the styles of Neoclassicism and Gothic Revival.

Eiffel Tower

Crystal Palace

The Wainwright Building, St Louis

IMPACT OF NEW MATERIALS

Throughout the nineteenth century, materials, methods, manufacture and engineering advanced rapidly. The Industrial Revolution affected the movement of population into the city from rural communities, changing the way business and life in general were conducted. Increased industrialisation in the nineteenth century and the growth of cities placed new demands on architects. Factories were needed for the new working classes, as well as transportation and railway stations. With expanding populations, land became scarce and architects soon found that they needed to build higher.

You should understand that the first major change in building methods of the nineteenth century came about with the invention of cast iron and steel as a result of the Industrial Revolution. By 1855, it was possible to mass-produce steel for construction. When Joseph Paxton used cast iron and glass as the basic building materials for the Crystal Palace in 1851, he successfully applied new industrial processes to architecture. He showed that large areas of glass could be incorporated into an easily constructed cast iron frame.

Similarly, Gustave Eiffel produced the famous Eiffel Tower in Paris (1887–1889) demonstrating the possibility of building tall structures ever higher using the new process. Very soon after, steel became an essential material that would shape the look of modern architecture. Engineers and engineering were therefore influencing architecture's development.

When the French engineer Robert Maillart (1872–1940) began experimenting with concrete, a completely new range of possibilities for structure emerged. Maillart was the first engineer to sense that concrete structures could be efficient, economical and elegant. He used simple ideas of construction to create forms such as the open, three-hinged, hollow-box arch, the mushroom slab and the deck-stiffened arch. Maillart's designs revolutionised architectural construction and paved the way for the innovative design movements that followed.

Steel, concrete and industrial processes assisted the development of architecture in the twentieth century. One of the first architects to realise the full potential of these materials was the American architect Louis Sullivan.

The Wainwright Building is a 10-story, red-brick landmark office building in the centre of St Louis, Missouri. Built in 1891 and designed by Dankmar Adler and Louis Sullivan, it is among the first skyscrapers in the world. Sullivan used a steel frame and applied his intricate terra cotta ornament in vertical bands to emphasise the height of the building. Famously, Sullivan coined the phrase 'form follows function'.

TIP

Many twentieth century architects experimented with the expressive possibilities of concrete. Oscar Niemeyer, Le Corbusier and Alvar Alto are three very good examples for further study.

TIP

Markers will always credit you when you clearly show that you understand the context of changes in style, materials, mass production, processes and building methods: especially innovations which change architecture.

The two questions below could well be answered by selecting work from the series of different styles and movements which emerged at the turn of the nineteenth and twentieth centuries. Try creating written responses to them within the timeframe of the exam.

Discuss or select examples of two architects/environmental designers from two different periods or contrasting styles. Comment on the characteristics of their work and their importance as a whole.

or

Compare the work of two environmental or architectural designers. How successfully have they used style, materials and form?

New Styles, New Influences

ARTS AND CRAFTS

In the second half of the nineteenth century a number of British architects began to look beyond the great historical styles of the past and to more simple approaches to design. They looked at examples of what had grown up in the centuries before in country houses, farm houses and cottages. They came to believe in the simple use of honest materials and revived the natural craftsmanship that went into the construction of these houses.

William Morris was a great influence on the Arts and Crafts movement which included architects such as Philip Webb (1831–1915), Norman Shaw (1831–1912) and Charles Voysey (1857–1941). As was discussed in the previous chapter, Morris believed that the mass-production techniques of the Industrial Revolution had resulted in inferior products. He strongly endorsed the view that traditional craftsmanship was the most honest approach to building. A popular choice for both Higher and Intermediate 2 questions is the Red House which Morris designed along with Philip Webb.

Phillip Webb, The Red House (1859)

The choice of materials for the construction of the Red House was natural, local red brick. Webb drew on what was called 'vernacular architecture': using locally-sourced materials to create a design in tune with the building's surroundings. The details which he used included a steep, slated roof and gothic arches around the doorways and windows. The form of the building gives the impression that it has grown from the ground and it is at one with its country setting. Inside, local woods are used for every detail, again emphasising natural, honest craftsmanship.

The Arts and Crafts movement was important as it stressed the values of simply designed, handcrafted products to give a natural form to structures. However, the march of industrialisation, the growth of mechanisation and technology meant that this approach was not sustainable.

ART NOUVEAU

Art Nouveau, or 'New Art', architects reacted against the historical styles of the nineteenth century. The style still relied on traditional methods but was characterised by the use of sinuous curving and whiplash lines. This style often extended to the interior of the building.

Art Nouveau started in Belgium around 1892. The movement was very short lived; barely 15 years. In Belgium, Victor Horta developed a flowing style based on organic forms in his series of Hotels. The most important of these was the Solvay Hotel.

The Art Nouveau style quickly spread across Europe. In France, the architect Hector Guimard evolved the principles of Art Nouveau into a coherent style. A good example is his Maison Coilliot of 1897. The combination of volcanic rock, cast iron and ceramics made by the owner Coilliot into a façade of decorative, swirling motifs causes the structure to make its presence known among the other, more traditional residences in the area.

Social and industrial developments made Art Nouveau a luxury style. Its emphasis on hand-crafted products meant that it was affordable only to the very wealthy. The two most popular Art Nouveau architects to use for Art and Design Studies are Antonio Gaudi and Charles Rennie Mackintosh.

Gaudi's work is to be found mainly in Barcelona, Spain. He worked almost in isolation from the other architects of the Art Nouveau style. Gaudi took this style to an extreme of exaggeration. He would start with a rough plan of what he wanted to design and then let it grow. Banded brickwork, multicoloured tiles, glass, wrought iron work, raw textures and materials and exaggerated forms were all features of his designs.

Gaudi believed in working free of all constraints except the mechanical conditions of the building. The sources he used to inspire exaggerated Art Nouveau forms in his work came from varying places, including animals, plants and geologic features. This is what gives his work the appearance of abstract forms interplaying with each other.

Casa Battlo is a very good example to show his importance. The apartment block has extravagant, twisted wrought iron balconies on the exterior which break up the surface and give real sculptural form. Inside and out, there is hardly a straight line used. Gaudi's life work was the cathedral of the Sagrada Familia which is still being added to today.

Far Left: *Casa Battlo*

Left: *Sagrada Familia*

Like Gaudi, **Charles Rennie Mackintosh** created a highly individual and original style. His designs are mainly found in his home city of Glasgow. A walking tour of the city shows Mackintosh's designs on architectural features such as window and door grates, as well as glass window panes and wrought iron fencing.

He was able to combine modern approaches to design with what he liked of Art Nouveau and the Arts and Crafts movement. A key difference is his move away from the excessive curves of Art Nouveau. Though he did incorporate some of his wife's floral elements into his work, linear line is a more distinctive feature of his work.

Mackintosh drew from a wider range of sources than mainstream Art Nouveau, looking to Japanese architecture and, importantly, his own Scottish heritage. Old fortified houses and the style of baronial castles and houses found all over Scotland were strong influences. The Glasgow School of Art (1897–1909) is a very good example of his work to use as an example in your essay.

In the main body of an essay you should show your knowledge of working methods, approaches and influences in your selected example. The arrows in the sample below show you where a marker would credit you in this very good analysis of an architecture example.

The Glasgow School of Art is Mackintosh's most important work. It represents the mature Mackintosh style.◀ It was designed as a working school for art students. The north side of the building overlooks the main street. The form of the building reflects its function as a School of Art.◀ The large grid-like window areas on the north side of the building are specially designed to provide light for the artist studios.◀ The eaves of the building project from the roofline to make the light even and the building is set back from the street to allow light into the basement studios.◀ Mackintosh uses materials in a decorative and functional way. For example, the ornamental brackets give extra support to the large window frames.◀

Mackintosh skilfully uses rectangles, verticals, and horizontals in the design of the building◄ as well as using Art Nouveau motifs taken from plant and vegetable forms to add interest to the exterior.◄

The building is sited on a steep slope. Mackintosh used the slope to emphasise the vertical composition of the west side of the building.◄ To add mass and form to the structure, he used projecting windows which run to the full height of the building.◄ The window frames are small and grid like. Doorways are used to provide deep recesses in the structure and emphasise form.◄

ART DECO

Art Deco was a decorative style made popular between 1920 and 1940. Architects working in this style adopted the modern construction methods of concrete, steel, chrome, glass and plastic. They incorporated geometric forms and striking colours, drawing inspiration from Oriental, Ancient Egyptian and South American architecture.

The style became popular for cinemas and some domestic architecture. In the USA, the style was adopted for large-scale skyscrapers. A very good example to use in your exam response is the Chrysler Building, built between 1928 and 1930. Originally only meant to be a modest office building, Mr. Chrysler had a change of heart and asked William van Allen to design the world's tallest building. In order to beat competitors attempting the same thing, van Allen designed a segmented, 185-foot spire to be fitted on the top. At its completion, the Chrysler Building became the world's largest man-made structure, overtaking the Eiffel Tower in Paris.

The lobby's interior is designed with different marbles, onyx and amber into Egyptian motifs along with frescoes depicting the Chrysler assembly line. Its exterior boasts extensive metalwork in the shapes of automobile parts like hubcaps, car fenders and hood ornaments. Once the tallest building in the world, the Chrysler Building is now as synonymous with New York City as the Empire State Building.

ACTIVITY

What key features contribute to the distinctive appearance of the Chrysler Building?

What other factors would van Allen have taken into account when designing this tall structure in the heart of a city? What is your opinion of the Art Deco style of the Chrysler building?

Chrysler Building, New York

MODERNISM

Improvements to construction methods continued and allowed architects to build even higher, evolve more complex structures and use extensive glass. A key to understanding the Modernist architecture that began to emerge in the early twentieth century is how industrial processes and the machine-age affected architects. In Modernist architecture there is a heavy emphasis on geometric form and in seeing that the machine as well as the craftsman could fashion highly attractive structures. This was known as the 'machine aesthetic'.

There is still much debate about what Modern architecture is exactly, but it is generally agreed that the movement has been fuelled by industrial development and technology. Often, this has translated into buildings that have clean, sharp lines, lots of glass and little to no ornamentation. Critics of the style have called it 'sterile', 'ossified' and 'lacking in meaning'.

BAUHAUS

Bauhaus, the common term for Staatliches Bauhaus, was formed in the city of Weimar, Germany in 1909. It is a German expression meaning 'house of building' or 'building school'. Walter Gropius (1883–1969) established Bauhaus as a teaching school for architecture and art. When the school moved to the city of Dessau it became an opportunity for Gropius to use new ideas that were to have a lasting effect on architecture.

If you decide to use Bauhaus in an essay, you should show that you understand their ideas about design. Some of the important points are as follows:

- A central idea of Bauhaus architects and designers was to do away with decoration.

- They wanted to develop and use a 'machine aesthetic' from new materials, like steel and concrete, plate glass and mass production processes.

- The Bauhaus building at Dessau was the first expression of these ideas.

- The Dessau building has a curtain wall over the exposed skeleton of steel structure which places strict emphasis on function with no decoration.

All this might seem commonplace today but this just underlines the importance of Bauhaus. The Bauhaus school lasted only from 1919 to 1933. In this short period it represented a break from the past and pointed the way to the future in architecture and design. One of the most famous examples of the style is the glass and bronze Seagram Building in New York, designed by Ludwig Mies van der Rohe with Philip Johnson.

Seagram Building, New York (1958)

TIP

If you are studying Higher, an historical knowledge of movements such as Art Nouveau, Art Deco and Arts and Crafts can help you recognise particular styles.

TIP

In Part B questions at both Higher and Intermediate 2, you are very often asked to comment on the designer's use of materials or working methods, style, sources of inspiration and who would wear the piece. At Higher you will also have to recognise the importance of the designer to the development of jewellery design.

As always, it is a good idea to focus on designers who are known, historically important and who have contributed to the development of jewellery.

DOES IT LOOK GOOD?

These are factors to do with the look or aesthetics of the piece. How well a piece of jewellery looks is a combination of all the visual elements, craftsmanship and the characteristics of the materials used to make it. Answering this question will include describing the impact of visual elements such as the mood and expression created by colour combinations of different materials, and the pattern and texture of the materials and their contribution to the appearance of the piece. At all times you can use these as reasons to explain why the piece functions well and/or helps to make it appealing to the intended users.

The visual elements can help you to evaluate the impact of a particular piece and give you an opportunity to share your personal opinion on it. Personal expression is very much a part of the appeal of jewellery. It helps if you can respond to a piece of jewellery by referring to what it expresses. Lively, glamorous, trendy, exciting, hot, cold, hard, sharp, soft, functional, comfortable, cheerful: all of these can be used to describe the overall expression of the jewellery and give you the opportunity to state strong opinions backed up with solid reasons.

OVERVIEW OF JEWELLERY DESIGN

As with other design areas it is a good idea to show that you understand how jewellery design developed. The craft of the jeweller is centuries old. Throughout history, precious metals like gold and silver have been used, along with materials such as diamond, gemstones and pearl, to create jewellery. Gold in particular has always been a popular material as it is rare, does not fade and is easy to work with.

Since ancient Egyptian, Greek and Roman times, jewellers used the properties of emeralds, garnets, amethysts and pearls to make highly coloured necklaces, bracelets, armlets, rings earrings, head ornaments and brooches. Coloured stones, glass, agates, crystal and enamel added to the wide range of sought-after materials for the jeweller. In many ways, the quality of a piece of jewellery was determined by the richness of the materials used. The skill of the jeweller was mainly about enclosing the precious materials in a suitably formed shape to suit the wearing requirements.

There has only ever been a limited supply of very precious materials. As early as the thirteenth century there were recipes for imitation pearls, and coloured glass was widely used as a substitute for some gemstones. Jaquin of Paris patented a method of making fake pearls which was to make Paris the main producer for over 200 years.

Paste jewellery was another form of faking the look of precious materials. Through this method, just about any fake gem could be produced. By the mid nineteenth century it was possible to mass-produce certain forms of jewellery using widely available imitation precious materials.

As in other design areas, jewellers in the nineteenth century looked to the past and to different cultures for sources of inspiration.

ARTS AND CRAFTS JEWELLERY

Arts and Crafts, Art Nouveau and Art Deco were design movements that affected many aspects of design, including jewellery. It is possible to trace similar influences through all six areas of design in Art and Design Studies.

The Arts and Crafts movement led by William Morris was a reaction against the sometimes inferior quality of mass-produced and machine made products that began to emerge during the Industrial Revolution (see Product, Architecture and Interior Design). Arts and Crafts jewellery designers used hand-tooled methods to promote a simpler look and feel to the jewellery they produced. They drew inspiration from natural forms and the symbols of Celtic Art.

Some selection is necessary for you to acquire enough background information to deal with an exam question sufficiently. Archibald Knox and CR Ashbee are two of the most important jewellery designers associated with Arts and Crafts.

Archibald Knox (1846–1933) is a good example of a jewellery designer who started working in the Arts and Crafts manner and later adopted the Art Nouveau style. Knox produced modern shape designs adapted from traditional Celtic motifs like intricate knot work and stylised animals. CR Ashbee (1863–1942) used similar organic forms.

Now try this...

Look at the two examples of Knox and Ashbee. Identify and comment on their sources of inspiration, how and when the pieces would be worn and who would be likely to wear them?

 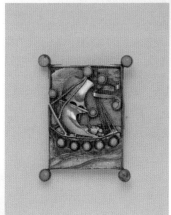

Knox Pendant   *Ashbee brooch*

ART NOUVEAU

One of the most popular choices at both Higher and Intermediate 2 is Art Nouveau jewellery. It is a good choice for Part B questions as there are known and important jewellery designers associated with the movement.

Again you should select important designers such as Rene Lalique, Louis Comfort Tiffany and Jean Fouquet. As with similar developments in Architecture and Interior Design, Art Nouveau jewellery has the familiar curving and sinuous lines. The sources of inspiration are natural, animal and organic forms.

The French designer Rene Lalique (1860–1945) is an acknowledged master of Art Nouveau jewellery. In a response to a Part B question it is a good idea to show that you have researched the background of the pieces you have selected and you are able to demonstrate the importance of your selected designer.

EXAMPLE

Rene Lalique was the leading figure of Art Nouveau jewellery.

Lalique began working as an apprentice to the Parisian jeweller Louis Aucoc. Within a short time, he set up as an independent jeweller in Paris in 1885. His work includes rings, expanding bracelets, medallions, brooches and buckles. Lalique created an entirely new approach to Jewellery and changed long established practices. He was one of the first Studio or Art designers making one-off pieces.◄ Lalique rejected the idea that jewellery should be made only of precious materials like diamond and gold.◄

Lalique introduced non-precious materials such as horn, bone and wood and developed working methods using glass, enamel, ivory and semi-precious stones.◄ Lalique especially loved the ever-changing glow of opals.

He influenced a generation of designers. Modern jewellery designers use many different precious, semi-precious and non-precious (even recycled) materials to create pieces which show Lalique's lasting influences and importance.?

(◄ indicates a point worthy of 1 mark)

At both Higher and Intermediate 2, the Part A question often asks about sources of inspiration.

Select two jewellery designers from different periods and discuss how they used different sources of inspiration and materials to create unique pieces. One part of this question could be answered with reference to Lalique. What were Lalique's sources of inspiration?

Lalique's sources of inspiration were fantasy creatures, insects and the human form.◄ He also used twisting vines and plants. In his works he often represented all the cycles of life from birth to death and decay.◄ He was also inspired by the qualities of the wide range of previously unused materials and the possibilities of processes such as enamelling.◄ He drew inspiration from looking at oriental jewellery, particularly Japanese.?

As with every essay, you need to show that you can evaluate examples of the jewellers work.

The dragonfly was one of Lalique's favourite motifs. The corsage is probably Lalique's most memorable work. It shows clearly his links to the Art Nouveau style, the range of materials that he worked with and the methods which allowed him to produce such a delicate and intricate piece.◄

The links to Art Nouveau are seen in the use of sweeping curves and the reference to natural forms.◄ Lalique's inspiration comes from human and insect forms combined with mythical beasts.◄

The huge wings are made of gold with glowing enamel inlays of plique-a-jour, making it look like stained glass when it catches the light.◄ The long insect like tail is decorated with Chrysoprase and clearly shows Lalique's imaginative use of non precious materials along with expensive one's like gold.◄ The corsage gives the appearance of a creature being born form the body of a fantasy creature and links the inspiration to themes of birth which Lalique favoured.◄ The arms of the creature are transformed into delicate spreading wings.◄ The golden claws add weight to the overall design.◄

The work suggests splendour and richness. It would probably have been designed as a one off for a special occasion and worn by a wealthy person.◄ However, the size and weight of the piece may suggest that it was uncomfortable for the user.◄

Rene Lalique, Dragonfly Woman corsage (1898)

(◄ At least one mark at Higher)

An evaluation like this would cover sources of inspiration use of materials and design issues such as wearability, visual impact and fitness for purpose. Many of the points made could be used to form a very good response at Intermediate 2.

Charles Louis Tiffany (1812–1902) founded Tiffany & Co. in New York in 1837. It started as a fancy goods store but grew quickly as it acquired a reputation for fine craftsmanship.

Like Lalique, Tiffany was passionate about nature. Many of his designs contain organic motifs inspired by natural forms close to his own home. His Dragonfly brooch gives an interesting comparison of the approaches of the two designers. Tiffany used the sinuous and delicate lines of Art Nouveau and combined several

Louis Comfort Tiffany, Dragonfly brooch (1904)

THE MAKERS OF FASHION – INNOVATION

In just about every question the main part of your response will deal with how your selected designers have used new ideas, methods, materials, and sources of inspiration to innovate and change fashion.

In a Part B question at Higher you might find a reference to innovation such as:

What important changes did they make to fashion design? Show how they have experimented with new and/or unusual materials and working methods.

At Intermediate 2 you might be asked to compare the use of materials by two fashion designers. If you have studied the changes in Fashion and Textiles you can include a section like this in your essay:

EXAMPLE

Innovation in fashion is necessary to meet consumer demands.◄ Predicting consumer demands is hard for the designer as tastes are seasonal and 'looks' in fashion shift very quickly.◄

In the twentieth century the challenge of innovation has meant the search for new technologies, for mass-production and new synthetic materials.◄ For example, the invention of Rayon led to the development and wide spread use of Nylon. Faster production lines meant that Nylon could be used for many fashion items very cheaply.◄

In the 1950s polyester was developed from the petrochemical industry. As a result Terylene became a widely-used synthetic material for fashion.◄

In the 1960s thermoplastic materials like PVC and Lycra became available.

Kevlar a very hard wearing carbon-based material and Gore-Tex are recent additions to the range of durable and highly functional materials used in practical outdoor and sportswear.◄

Moulded plastics, heat reactive fabrics and laser-produced fabric which change colour mean that today, the range is vast.◄

(◄ at least one mark at Higher and more at Intermediate 2)

Most of the important fashion makers were innovative. Your choice of designers should really be based on those designers who have contributed most to the development of fashion.

At both levels you need to consider fashion designers that will allow you to discuss, comment on and compare the design issues identified in the question.

Unlike interior design, architecture and jewellery, it would be difficult to base a fashion essay on one of the great movements, for example Bauhaus or Art Nouveau. It is better to identify individual designers or fashion houses that had a lasting influence. Then, if you like, you can show how they were influenced by or reflected the design movements of the time. The most important designers to select are the real makers of fashion, those whose inventiveness have helped to shape fashion as a whole. It also helps to note any response of theirs to emerging social trends.

TIP

Break up the twentieth century into periods of one and/or two decades. This makes it easier to identify the major innovations, influences and important fashion makers.

Part B questions at Higher require you to select important designers from different periods. Most of the rapid developments took place in the twentieth century.

1900–1910

When Paul Poiret produced a corset-free, high-waisted dress in 1906 he began a trend in fashion bringing garments closer to the natural shape of the body.

The social position of women in the nineteenth century dictated that the corset should be worn tightly around a woman's waist and that dresses should be long so as not to reveal anything of the woman's legs apart from the ankles. Poiret developed designs for simple dresses in straight classic lines with graceful folds that were very different from the lined, highly decorated and lace-filled type popular at the time. He discarded petticoats and crinoline undergarments which also hid the natural lines of a woman's form.

fancy dress costume (1911)

Poiret opened fashion to influences from the art movements of the time. He took the vivid colours of the Fauve and geometric forms of Cubist artists and adapted oriental influences and designs from the ballet to enrich his own work. Up until Poiret's time, fashion designers had used live models in their salons to display their work. He recognised the importance of window display and began for the first time to use wooden dummies to show off his work. The fancy dress costume of vibrant, glowing, shimmering colours, with beaded embellishments shows many of the characteristics that made Poiret outstanding.

Poiret is important to the development of fashion. Using Poiret in an essay will allow you to discuss important changes in fashion in response to social change, changes in materials, technology and new methods of producing and marketing fashion to target groups.

1910–1920

Social change and innovation went hand in hand in the early part of the twentieth century. During this period the place of women in society changed. This is important for your understanding of the development of fashion. Prior to the twentieth century women were rarely educated to a high level. Only the very rich could afford fashion and this was reflected in the styles of the nineteenth century. The First World War gave women opportunities to enter the world of work. After the war, women achieved the vote and continued to emerge as wage earners in their own right.

An outstanding designer at the heart of this change was Gabrielle 'Coco' Chanel. Chanel opened her Paris fashion house in 1914. She was quick to recognise the changes taking place in society. Chanel noticed that women liked the woollen cardigans worn by soldiers in the war. She saw the possibility of using jersey, a woollen material mainly used at the time for men's underwear, in her work. New forms of knitting had been developed at the time allowing Chanel to seize the opportunity to create simpler lines and craft a style with expertly cut and finished short skirts and cardigan jackets. Her 'Garconne' (boyish) look had huge appeal.

Chanel's 'Little Black Dress' became a standard item in women's wardrobes. It was functional and could be made to suit the individual by the use of accessories. 'Coco' Chanel was an important fashion maker and innovator because she introduced simple, elegant, relaxed and functional clothes that articulated the aspirations of women in the early twentieth century. She adapted ideas and materials from men's clothes to create stylish garments for modern women.

Chanel revolutionised high fashion by completely replacing the traditional corset with the comfort and casual elegance of simple suits and dresses made of unpretentious materials. Chanel thought it was important to recognise function in women's fashion. Her fashion design reflected the times and at the same time pointed to the future.

After the First World War, fashion developed in new directions. The corset had gone and women's fashion was more directed towards showing the form of the body. The Chanel style is still around today.

Gabrielle 'Coco' Chanel, day ensemble (1927)

Now try this...

Compare Coco Chanel with Vivienne Westwood or Katharine Hamnett.

Write a general introduction which tells the reader why you have selected them, and how changes in society and innovation affect fashion. Then analyse examples of their works which show this. In your conclusion, briefly state two things about each designer which show their importance.

Tip

Westwood designed in the Punk Era where street-style and politics influenced fashion.

Hamnett is very concerned about sustainable and eco-friendly production methods and her designs reflect this.

Chanel designed just after the First World War when there were changes in society affecting women.

1920–1930

Throughout the decade of the 'Roaring Twenties', dance crazes, the silent movies, the Art Deco style of the time and the rise of the fashion magazine created new markets for the expanding world of fashion. New man-made fibres and production lines were available. In 1913, the zipper was invented opening up further possibilities. Rayon was created and was widely used as a replacement for expensive silk in the form of Nylon. Important fashion innovators from this period whose work influenced the development of fashion were Madeleine Vionnet, Elsa Schiaparelli and Mariano Fortuny.

Madeleine Vionnet's interest was in the trade and craft of fashion. Having a background as a dressmaker enabled her to exploit the way she cut fabrics to emphasise the curves and gestures of the woman's body. One of her major innovations was the creation of the bias cut, where fabric is cut diagonally across the warp and weft threads. Bias-cut garments have a very different look from ordinary garments.

Cutting patterns along the bias forces the fabric to cling to the body and move with it. This created Vionnet's trademark look of draped, form-conscious clothing with flowing lines and draped fabrics which enabled women to look more feminine and move gracefully without the constraint of the corset.

The bias cut was a new method of construction in fashion technique and allowed for new looks. In applying the bias cut to her designs, Vionnet first divided up the body along the lines of waist, shoulders and breasts and then united the lines with woman's shape. She used simple combinations of draping and minimal seams to solve the problem of form and function.

Vionnet was important because she integrated comfort and movement into design for the first time, as well as form and cut. The result was very elegant, body-clinging designs. Vionnet's bias cut approach has had a lasting effect on the development of fashion.

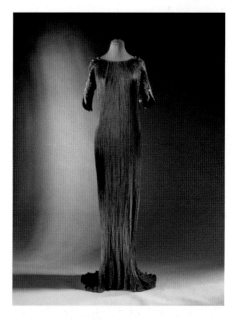

Fortuny, pleated dress

Madeleine Vionnet, evening gowns (1939)

Now try this...

Compare Vionnet or Fortuny with contemporary designers such as Issey Miyake or John Galliano. These are good choices as contemporary designers were influenced by Vionnet and Fortuny.

In your introduction, write about the importance of the use of fabric (materials). Analyse examples to show how Vionnet used the bias cut to create elegant, form-clinging dresses or how Fortuny used pleating. Show how Miyake uses a similar approach but to different effect. Use some biographical information but remember that most of the marks will come from your response to the question not how much you know about the designer's life. In your conclusion, as well as commenting on the lasting influence of the bias cut or Fortuny's methods, comment on how Vionnet or Fortuny influenced future designers.

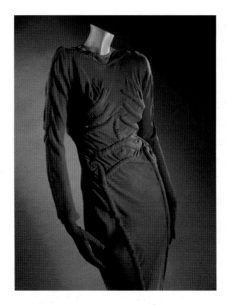

Two dresses by Elsa Schiaparelli

Elsa Schiaparelli was one of the leading fashion innovators and makers throughout the 1920s and 30s. She was the first to use the padded shoulder in her designs. Among her many sources of inspiration were the Surrealist artists of the time especially Salvador Dali.

Her fashion collections were always based on imaginative themes such as the circus, art and butterflies. Like other great innovators, Schiaparelli changed the look of fashion. Her clever use of cut squared the shoulders, slightly rounded the bosom and narrowed the waist. She exploited new synthetic fabrics and incorporated the zipper into her work. Schiaparelli introduced wit and invention into her designs and made extensive use of appliqué to enliven and personalise her creations.

Now try this...

Write a comparison of Schiaparelli or Fortuny with a designer such as Zandra Rhodes or Jean Paul Gaultier who use varied sources of inspiration and target new markets. Write about the sources of inspiration of these designers and show that they are all influenced by various art forms.

Fortuny's importance was his invented method of pleating. He used a heat process to make the dense layers of pleat permanent, then arranged them in a unique way so that the dress clung and floated about a woman's body, thus emphasising the elegant form.

A good example to refer to in an essay is the Delphos gown. It was a column of pleated silk based on the robes seen on Ancient Greek statues. The effect made a woman look elongated.

1930–1950

Fashion has different purposes. The things we wear can be used to attract, represent power and influence, adorn ceremonious events and performances and, of course, protect against the elements. Great changes in fashion have come about as the result of political and social change – no more so than during war times. The Second World War was a period of shortage and rationing and a 'make

TIP

Schiaparelli was influenced by Surrealist art. Fortuny was influenced by ancient Greek art. Rhodes was influenced by the ethnic art of different cultures.

do and mend' attitude prevailed. Fashion during the war years was limited to producing utility-type clothing with a unisex aesthetic. At the end of the war, however, there was a sudden demand to put glamour and elegance back into fashion.

In 1947, the French designer Christian Dior presented a collection of wasp-waisted, rounded shoulders and hip-padded designs for day wear. The New Look created a very elegant silhouette and was so important that it set the direction for fashion design in the 1950s. Dior's New Look came just after the austerity and utility of the Second World War which had made women's fashion almost military looking. The style was deliberately luxurious and feminine.

One of his most successful innovations was to build all the support and control needed in his gowns so that neither a brassiere nor a corset was required. Woman's dresses with rounded shoulders, high bust and very full skirt, gloves and high heel shoes completed the look. Like other innovators he used newer synthetic material and explored their possibilities in his designs. Fashion design throughout this period continued to be glamorous and elegant.

Christian Dior, 'Carolle' or 'figure 8', a name that suggested the silhouette of the New Look with its prominent shoulders, accentuated hips and small waist (Spring 1947)

> ### TIP
>
> *A good comparison to make could be with the Spanish fashion designer Cristobal Balenciaga. When fashion trends were tending more and more towards ready-to-wear fashion, Balenciaga remained the master of high fashion. It was really his masterful cutting and sewing technique and his awareness of making light easy to wear dresses that makes him a great innovator.*

1950–1970

The fashion innovators in this period were again responding to changes in society, materials and manufacture. Fashion began to reflect street styles. Movie stars were trend setters. People, especially teenagers, had more money to spend and the range of materials available to fashion expanded to include denim, Lycra, metals and man-made fibres. It is important to remember that, at this time, high fashion was still the main market for the fashion makers.

Early in the 1960s Yves Saint Laurent opened his Rive Gauche shop in Paris with new fashion drawn from pop art, street styles and, importantly, ready-to-wear. The Prêt-à-Porter became the main target market for the leading designers. This was a time when an ever expanding market was looking for very good quality ready-to-wear fashion. This was an era of mass media, mass consumption and globalisation. Yves Saint Laurent (YSL) became an international brand, introducing chic glamour into fashion.

In the 1960s the young were an emerging market of fashion consumers who had ever-increasing freedom and buying power. Young people's income was at its highest since the end of the Second World War, creating the desire for a wardrobe which did more than simply copy adult dress. Clothes aimed specifically at young people, which Mary Quant had been designing since the late 1950s, became popular. London was the style capital of the world for 'trendy gear' in the 'Swinging Sixties'; the tastes and preferences of young people began to drive innovation.

Shops played an important part in popularising new fashions. Whole areas of London like King's Road and Carnaby Street were transformed as boutiques took over. Boutiques sold an inexpensive range of rapidly changing outfits and offered an informal atmosphere and self-service, unlike traditional clothes shops. This period saw the emergence of both the fashion boutiques of Bazaar, Biba, Chelsea Girl and Laura Ashley and the designer emporiums of Armani, Benetton and Fiorucci. Instead of buying outfits designed for specific occasions or times of the day, people preferred separates. Boutiques were created by young designers who made the kind of fashion their friends wanted and sold cheap ready-to-wear garments instead of haute couture, while emporiums controlled their brand and tried to establish consumer loyalty to their trademark styles.

During this period innovation and change was rapid. Social change had quickened, too. Fashion began to reflect pop music and street culture, space travel, Flower Power, Beatniks, Teddy boys, Mods and Rockers and embraced globalisation. Fashion textile designers celebrated the modern age. Space-age silver was mixed with primary-coloured prints taken from Pop and Op Art. Novel fashion materials were introduced, including shiny, wet-look PVC, easy-care acrylics and polyesters.

Of all the designers of this period, Mary Quant was in tune with youthful consumers who sought a personally defined look. Trends were being created by the consumer and Quant was able to interpret them in fashion. In her work she used simple shapes with abstract patterns and bold, flat colours. She took advantage of new materials such as Lurex to create tights with an array of different patterns. These showed off the exposed legs of those who wore the increasingly-shortened mini skirt.

Quant is important because she successfully brought together art and fashion, fashion and popular culture, and craft and marketing to create a unique brand which was very much in tune with the swinging pop and youthful culture of the 1960s. Quant is credited with the invention of the mini-skirt, which was the most eye-catching garment of the decade. Designed for an ideally skinny female form, it was one of the most significant innovations of the period.

Zandra Rhodes was firstly a textile designer and this has influenced her approach to design. She has drawn inspiration over her career from the shapes of clothing in different cultures. Her clothes were initially designed to transform the wearer into a world of fantasy. Her first fashion collection in 1969 was shown in the period of hippie culture and rebellious youth.

Rhodes has a very personal approach to the process of designing. As a textile designer, she recognises the potential of print to enhance a garment. Rhodes allows the design to follow the shapes of her textile prints. Her method involves drawing patterns out then laying the fabric on top before it is cut out in the shape of the garment.

This was a fresh approach to the construction of clothing and dressmaking in the period that did not follow the rules of pattern cutting and dressmaking of haute couture. Her work is spontaneous and arises from her constant sketching and researching.

TIP

If you choose designers from this period you should be able to include aspects of Sixties culture. For that reason, two designers really stand out.

Mary Quant and Zandra Rhodes both responded in different ways to the sweeping changes of the Swinging Sixties and the age of Flower Power.

Mary Quant dress

Mary Quant and Coco Chanel are two contrasting designers from different periods who were influential in the development of fashion.

Write an essay to show and compare their distinctive approaches.

Keep in mind the following:

- Both designed for a new markets following social change.
- Both radically changed the shape of clothing.
- Both used new methods and materials.
- Both produced classic garments (the Garconne look and the mini skirt) that had a lasting influence.
- Both are from different historical periods.
- Give your own opinion.

1970–1990

The 1970s was an anything-goes decade. Fashion design became more about making a personal identity statement. As with other periods, innovations came from new materials, technologies and what was happening in the world of media, music, the street, politics and the environment.

Designers freely borrowed from all sorts of historical, traditional, ethnic and street styles. This was called Post-modernism. More than ever before, young people dressed to shock, impress and to create their own fashion identity. The succession of street styles begun in the 1950s has continued to thrive. We now have Chavs and Japanese street styles of the early twenty-first century.

In this period there was almost a supermarket of different styles. Punks ripped apart second-hand clothing picked up in charity and army surplus stores and accessorised them with pins, razor blades and badges. The Ravers from the club scene in the 1990s used beachwear, science fiction costume and ghetto glamour to create their personal expression and accessorised with tattoos and body piecing. It is against this background that you can use the most important radical designers as they responded to the rapid changes taking place on the street, in the music scene and in the media.

TIP

If you study this period there are many recognised designers. Make your choice on how well they fit the likely design issues set in the questions. If you can't, don't use them. In your introduction set the context by referring to the changes taking place in consumer tastes and street fashion.

In the 1970s and 1980s, Vivienne Westwood and Katharine Hamnett used fashion design to make a statement. This allowed target users to fully identify with the social, political and environmental issues raised by both.

In the 1970s Westwood established a partnership with music producer Malcolm McLaren, the originator of Punk. They opened a shop in 1971 called Let it Rock. The shop became an outlet for Westwood's very challenging ideas about fashion. Westwood used a huge range of different materials and drew on an equally wide range of historical styles. In her work she made underwear as outerwear, reviving the corset, and inventing the mini-crini. When she changed the name of her shop to Seditionaries she began to shape a very unconventional style using things like ripped garments, 1950s stars, leather, chains and badges, straps and buckles reflecting the street Punk style.

Katharine Hamnett, another prominent designer of the time, sought to make fashion environmentally friendly. She was concerned about the sweat-shop approach to producing clothing in the developing world and refused to use materials that had petrochemicals or pesticides. This led her to use organic and recyclable materials in her fashion design.

Vivienne Westwood, fashion in motion

Hamnett's innovation has been in the way she created new styles and trends in fashion such as power dressing, the military and utilitarian look, stretch-denim, garment dying and retro. She used ideas from working-men's clothing such as boiler suits and trench coats, and brought in bubble skirts and low waist jeans. In her 2006 design collection 'E' she used organically grown cottons and wools to create her slogan T-shirts. Hamnett's approach is fashion with a social and political conscience.

> ### Tip
>
> *If you choose to write about Hamnett you may argue against her view on the use of environmentally-friendly materials in your conclusion and take the view that the whole point of fashion is that it is wasteful (e.g. buy clothes that we don't need and then throw them away because we want the latest style).*

French designer Christian Lacroix made his mark on the international fashion world in the 1980s. His design themes were inspired by historical costume. He drew on an immense range of sources including the circus and ancient civilisations; the final result often being luxurious. Lacroix reintroduced the bustle and used lacing, padding, complex layers of trimming, embroidery, vivid colours and patterns to create eye-catching contrasts in his work

Hamnett's 'No War' slogan T-shirt

Jean Paul Gaultier, also from France, was established as an international fashion designer by the late 1970s. He had worked as a design assistant with Cardin where he established himself. Gaultier's influences were the street life of Paris, artistic rebellion, film theatre and music. One of his most famous works was the corset-style bustier worn by Madonna for her Blond Ambition world tour of 1990. Like Westwood, Gaultier broke the established rules using underwear as outerwear. Gaultier blurred the sexes and played with proportion, turning fashion upside down and inside out.

Japanese fashion designer Issey Miyake is a popular choice for Higher and Intermediate 2. Unlike Hamnett and Westwood his approach does not make a political or social statement. Instead, his designs are almost like sculpture. In a career which spanned nearly four decades he has been a constant innovator. He aims to use a single piece of cloth to create very diverse forms of clothing.

Innovation for Miyake is about the manipulation of fabric itself. He called his first ever fashion show 'A Poem in Cloth and Stone'.

Miyake aims to stimulate imagination through his design. He designs around the body almost as if he is using it as a support for the flowing sculptural shapes that he creates. In the 1970s and 80s he used new fabrics such as polyester, jersey, acrylic and wool. Miyake uniquely combined traditional Japanese ideas with mass-production techniques and craft skills. Using these materials in new ways, he created highly expressive surface effects on textiles and combined function and comfort with sheer craft.

In 1993 he introduced 'Pleats Please' which is a brand based on a light, flexible and permanently pleated fabric. Miyake's approach was first to construct a garment and add pleating at the end stages. The result is a rich combination of textured surfaces combined with flowing shapes and forms which make his work unique. His development of the pleating theory revolved around first sewing garments, then finishing them, and finally the pleating.

Miyake ensemble (1983)

Now try this...

Miyake's designs appear like sculptures, blurring the distinction between art and design. He is said to work like a sculptor using the abstract qualities of materials, pleating, twisting, shrinking and printing both natural and synthetic material to create designs which relate the form of the garment to the shape of the body.

Compare Miyake with a designer such as Elsa Schiaparelli who also worked as an artist and designer. Concentrate on their sources of inspiration, methods and materials.

or

Compare Miyake with Fortuny along similar lines.

1990 Onward

Throughout the 1990s specialised brands for fashion and accessories expanded. Versace, Armani, Cruise, Gap, Boss and Jigsaw all developed to possess strong consumer attraction. Alongside this growth, the catwalk designers tended to use fashion to challenge accepted views about style and taste in fashion. The leading innovators made fashion statements that used different combinations of historical styles and a range of technology. They broke the rules and conventions to shock, provoke, astonish and outrage people with radical ideas about design and create their own vivid personal visions. Much of the work of these radical designers has been theatrical and wildly glamorous – a trend that continues to this day.

Some designs seem to be more about showcasing the fantastic ideas of the designer rather than creating fully functional clothing for any particular target group of users. One radical group that did create a dedicated consumer group were Comme de Garcon. Rei Kawakubo was the founder and main designer of the group. In her work she appears to break all the rules using undergarments combined with outer garments, odd placement of fastenings, allowing fabric to billow where tightness is expected, half-dyeing completed garments and deliberately using things out of proportion.

John Galliano and Alexander McQueen are two contemporary designers who continue the idea of spectacle, provocation and outrage. If you choose either of these designers you can very quickly identify such design issues as function, target market, technology and aesthetics. They are designers who are inspired by a personal vision and, as a result, create wild theatrical fashion. Yet both designers have worked at the most important fashion houses of Givenchy and Dior, ensuring that their work displays the highest levels of craftsmanship. Both designers use the catwalk to show their great tailoring skills as well as showmanship, presentation skills and the exciting spectacle of high fashion.

ABOVE LEFT: John Galliano dress

ABOVE RIGHT: Alexander McQueen dress

John Galliano officially launched his own label in 1984. In 1995 he was appointed head designer at the great french fashion house of Givenchy. This meant that much of his work could be targeted at the very rich and famous. In his work he successfully combines influences from historical fashion styles of the past, like the bias cut, with a feel for using new materials and contemporary styling related to street fashion and popular culture. Galliano's importance lies in the way he is able to re-interpret romantic styles of the past to give them a contemporary feel.

Alexander McQueen followed on from Galliano at the fashion house of Givenchy and further developed the idea of the fashion show as a spectacular performance. Drawing on influences from contemporary artists such as Damien Hirst, McQueen created a collection in 1995 where the show took place within a giant transparent cube with snow drifts, blasted trees and ice to make it look like the set for the horror film *The Shining*. Themes of horror and extravagant spectacle are common in McQeens work. He uses fashion to provoke and make a statement and uses shock tactics to convey many of his radical ideas and views about fashion. He often uses themes to interpret historical events such as the 1998 show 'Highland Rape'. The theme of this show was the the violent actions of the English taken to suppress rebel Scots in the eighteenth century. The show featured blood-spattered, tartan-clad models wearing jackets and lace dresses that were ripped apart and wild hairstyles. The detail even included cuts and bruises to enhance the shock effect.

A Part B exam question could look something like this:

Select two fashion and/or textile designers working in different periods or styles that you think made an important contribution to fashion. With reference to examples of their work, explain why you think they were important designers.

In this example two highly contrasting designers (Chanel and McQueen) are selected from periods nearly 70 years apart.

> **TIP**
>
> *Your essay should include conclusions. Normally this will be at the end of the essay but you will be credited with drawing conclusions throughout the essay, as is the case in this example. The conclusion is where you should offer comment and opinion of the importance of your selected designers.*

Fashion design very much reflects changes in society. Two designers from different periods who reflected change were Coco Chanel and Alexander McQueen. Chanel reflected changes to the place of woman in society after the First World War and McQueen reflected the media-dominated world of the 1990s.◄

Coco Chanel was a French designer whose outfits have stood the test of time. Her 'little black dress' was made in 1926 and has become a standard item of women's attire up to the present day.◄ In its original form it was stylish enough for parties and yet formal enough to be worn at a funeral.◄ Since it was first made, it has been imitated by various designers. However, Chanel was the first to make this very functional dress which could be accessorised to suit any individual.◄ It captured the liberated, confident and elegant feeling that Chanel wanted women to show. It was an important change in fashion that freed women from stiff and heavy corsets and skirts which had been very conservative.◄ It allowed freedom of movement and expression.◄ Coco Chanel was one of the most influential and important fashion designers of the twentieth century. She used existing materials in new ways such as jersey and cardigan jackets. ◄ She herself was influenced by men's suits and sportswear to create her famous 'Garçonne' look.◄ Her contribution to fashion is born out of the fact that Chanel is still a major fashion house to this day producing similar lines which are simple, elegant and can be adapted to meet a wide range of functions. ◄ Clearly, Coco Chanel was a great innovator in fashion who adapted ideas from different sources to meet the aspirations of women whose place in society was changing. ◄

Alexander McQueen is a contemporary fashion designer who was born in London's East End. McQueen learnt his trade as a tailor on the famous Savile Row, which influenced his approach to quality tailoring and finish in his approach to fashion design.◄ Seventy years after Chanel opened her first fashion outlet, McQueen opened his. In 1996, he was approached to head up the team at the fashion house of Givenchy in Paris.◄

McQueen uses shock tactics to convey his radical ideas and views. McQueen became influential in the 1990s when the influence of the media reached new heights.◀ One of his most radical shows was 'Highland Rape' which was a theme taken from the violent repression of the Scots by the English. The show featured blood-spattered models with slashed clothes, ruffled hair styles and cuts and bruises.◀ The fact that McQueen's show was criticised for his shock tactics did not take away from the highly innovative approaches that he used.

McQueen's work is very flamboyant and theatrical.◀ Most of his creations are for special-effect catwalk shows.◀ However, McQueen is an important designer in that some of his radical approaches eventually influence the fashion designs of the High Street.◀ Even though his approaches are radical, the tailoring of his work is always of the highest quality.◀ He uses a wide range of sources of inspiration from contemporary society to historical themes which makes him one of the most important designers alive today. McQueen's work is not simply about outrage. Another, more beautiful and romantic, side to his work includes 'Ice Escapades', which was composed of ice-blues and silvers that made the work diamond-like, elegant and pure.

All of McQueen's work emphasises skilful cuts and stitching, which has increased his influence on other designers. McQueen's importance to fashion design is demonstrated most clearly by the fact that, having scandalised London in the 1990s and having shocked the fashion world on many occasions, McQueen is respected and has been the British Designer of the Year three times.

(◀ worthy of at least 1 mark at Higher)

The response would form the basis of a very good, high-scoring answer to the question.

FASHION ACCESSORIES

If you have been designing hats, bags, shoes or other fashion accessories in your practical work, it is acceptable to refer to these in Fashion and Textile Design exams. Many of the same issues of the use of technology and new materials, aesthetics and function apply equally to accessories such as shoes.

The twentieth century brought creative innovations in both design and materials used to make fashionable styles in shoes. The steel-reinforced stiletto heel first appeared on shoes in the mid twentieth century. Designers also incorporated plastics, zippers, Velcro and high-tech fibres into their footwear, with the line between functional, sporting styles and high fashion often blurred as a result.

Ankle-strap sandal designed by Ferragamo (1938)

Exam Preparation

In preparing for your exam you should look in detail at the work of at least **two** different fashion and/or textile designers. You should know their background thoroughly, including who influenced them. Find out, also, if they have been an influence on people who followed on, or in the development of fashion or textile design as a whole.

Do not limit your research to a couple of examples from each designer or movement. The better informed you are the more completely you will be able to answer the question paper. Remember that past papers are just a guide to the type of questions that have been asked in previous years. The examiners are always refining the style of question you may be asked. If you have a thorough knowledge of your subject you will be able to respond to changes in questioning.

When looking at fashion design we should attempt to understand how the designer approached the work and what his or her main concerns were, as well as the design issues that had to be solved. Use the question prompts below to get you started in your exam preparation.

Who made it? Do you know the name of the designer or anything about them? Previous knowledge often helps our appreciation of a piece of design.

When was it made? Knowing when a design was made can help our understanding of why it was created. The conditions of the time can have an effect on how the designer approached the task. Technological changes have, throughout history had an affect on how designers approached their work.

Who made it? Do you know the name of the designer or anything about them? Some knowledge of their background such as associations with fashion houses and when they lived can help set the context for your essay. Previous knowledge often helps our appreciation of a piece of design.

What is the purpose of the design? Who is the intended target market? Where is the garment or accessory likely to be worn? Consider whether the materials used suit the intended function of the design and how the item is meant to be worn.

How well does it look? Decide if the item has visual impact. Does it look good? What is your opinion of it?

Does it function well? How well does the garment do what it is meant to do? Would it be suitable for its intended function? Think about whether it could be worn easily and comfortably, as well as if it is safe. Has it been made with appropriate materials? Think, too, how well the various materials work with one another.

Use these questions and the ones you develop on your own to fully prepare yourself for the exam paper.

Movements and Styles in Art and Design

Arts & Crafts

A movement that came about as a reaction to the heavily ornamented styles of decoration that was common in the latter half of the nineteenth century. It was at its height between 1880 and 1910. The most prominent member of the movement was William Morris, the English artist and poet, who had been inspired by the writings of John Ruskin. Morris was critical of the mass production of goods that had followed on from the Industrial Revolution; he felt they were shoddy. Morris wanted the workers to have the opportunity to produce well-designed beautiful objects that reflected the talents of the people making them. Apart from Morris, other important designers of the movement included **Charles Robert Ashbee, Walter Crane, Phoebe Anna Traquair, Charles Rennie Mackintosh, Christopher Dresser, Edwin Lutyens, Frank Lloyd Wright, Gustav Stickley, Greene & Greene** and **Charles Voysey.**

Art Deco

A design movement of the 1920's and 1930's. The name came from the 1925 *Exposition Internationale des Arts Decoratifs Industriels et Modernes*, held in Paris, which showed new advances in design in the then modern world. It included most aspects of decorative design, such as jewellery, fashion, textile and graphics. Its influence on architecture can still be seen today in some remaining buildings of the period. Art Deco style was thought to be very elegant and used exotic materials in the production of many of its designs. The goods produced were often luxury items aimed at the expanding middle class market of the time. Its imagery took inspiration from machinery and streamlining (this was the beginning of the modern world we know today) and the art of ancient Egypt and Aztec Mexico (there were new discoveries being made about both cultures around this time). Many Art Deco works use either geometric patterns or flowing, streamlined shapes, suggesting speed. Notable designers of the movement included **Cassandre, Erte, Lalique, Eileen Gray**, and **Cartier.** Among the important architects of the period were **William van Alen** and **Raymond Hood.**

Art Nouveau

A design movement that lasted between 1890 and 1905. It developed mostly in France, Belgium, Austria, Spain, Britain and America. In Britain, where it grew from the Arts and Crafts movement, Glasgow was the main centre of its development. Although there were a variety of styles in different countries, Art Nouveau is usually identified by the use of 'whiplash', or undulating lines, in its designs. Art Nouveau designers tried to design complete environments where buildings, furniture, textiles, and all other decoration had a similarity of style. The works designed included graphic, jewellery, furniture, interior design and architecture. Important contributors to the movement included **Alphonse Mucha, Aubrey Beardsley, Antonio Gaudi, Charles Rennie Mackintosh, Hector Guimard, Rene Lalique** and **Louis Comfort Tiffany.**

Bauhaus

An extremely influential school of art, design and architecture established by Walter Gropious in Weimar, Germany in 1919. It only lasted for 14 years, being closed by the Nazis in 1933. During this time it moved to Dessau for a spell and finally to Berlin just before it closed. One of the school's aims was to bring art and design into everyone's life. Although influenced by the Arts and Crafts movement, the Bauhaus encouraged students to embrace the new materials of the time. Art and design history was not taught; instead students were encouraged to experiment with materials before producing designs that used the characteristics of the chosen materials to best effect. They developed prototypes for goods to be made using mass-production techniques. This can be seen in the cantilevered chairs designed by Marcel Breuer. The Bauhaus attracted an outstanding group of artists, architects and designers to teach its courses. They were some of the most important thinkers in their respective fields. **Walter Gropius**, **Ludwig Mies van der Rohe**, **Wassily Kandinsky**, **Lyonel Feininger**, **Paul Klee**, **Oskar Schlemmer**, **László Moholy-Nagy** and **Josef Albers** were all members of staff at one time or another. Once the school was closed, many Bauhaus teachers emigrated to the United States, where they either developed their professional practice or took up lecturing posts in a variety of universities.

Constructivism

An art movement developed in 1917 by the Russian sculptor Tatlin. The aim was to make abstract sculpture for an industrial society. The work used modern materials such as glass, plastics and steel. **Antoine Pevsner** in Paris and **Naum Gabo** in Germany were also important artists in the movement.

Cubism

Probably the most influential twentieth century art movement, Cubism lasted between 1907 and the early 1920s. Initially developed in art by Picasso and Braque, their idea of portraying the essence of a thing rather than the thing itself quickly spread to other creative forms, such as literature. It developed Cézanne's ideas about the expression of form and also drew inspiration from Fauvism and African art. In their work the artists' subject matter is broken up and reassembled, often showing multiple views of the same subject simultaneously. **Picasso, Braque** and **Gris** were the main Cubist artists.

Expressionism

Based in Germany and northern Europe between 1905 and 1925, Expressionists were concerned with portraying their feelings and emotions with regard to their subject. It was influenced by the work of van Gogh and Goya. Though the main artists involved are **Munch, Nolde, Roualt, Kirchner** and **Beckmann**, Expressionism has continued to influence and be used as an approach by many twentieth and twenty-first century painters, like **Willem de Kooning, Jackson Pollock, Jean-Michel Basquiat** and **David Hockney**.

Fauvism

An early twentieth century art movement renowned for its use of bright intense colours, often painted in a bold, seemingly uncontrolled manner. The term comes from the French word 'fauves' meaning 'wild beasts'. The main artists were **Matisse, Derain** and **Dufy**.

Futurism

A movement started in Italy in 1909. Its works celebrated the developing machine age and a number of the main paintings associated with it attempted to show movement. Futurists rejected harmony and good taste in art and chose to ignore all subjects dealt with traditionally, instead focussing on the unification of a subject with its surroundings. Among the most prominent artists associated with it were **Bella, Boccioni, Carra** and **Severini**.

High Tech

A term used to describe design that uses the latest advances in technology. It is often associated with the Information Technology, Robotics or aerospace industries. In architecture, it describes buildings built using the most up to date materials and techniques. One feature shared by most High Tech buildings is their construction using a steel frame (sometimes exposed on the outside of the building) and glass curtain walls. In others the services – lifts, heating and ventilation pipes etc. – are exposed on the outside of the building, leaving large uncluttered spaces within. Few High Tech buildings have any applied decoration because the patterns of the exposed framework and service piping provide ornamentation enough. Among the most prominent High Tech architects are **Norman Foster, Richard Rogers** and **Renzo Piano.**

Impressionism

Impressionism was an art movement that started in France in the 1860s. Impressionists were interested in showing the effects of light upon their chosen subjects. In order to do so they would paint the same subject at different times of day or during different seasons or weather conditions. Their paintings tried to show a particular moment in time and their subject matter came from modern times. Their ideas on composition were influenced by photography and Japanese art. Some of the most important Impressionists were **Monet, Pissarro, Degas** and **Renoir.**

Neoclassicism

An art movement based on the ideals of the ancient Greeks and Romans that took place from the mid eighteenth to mid nineteenth centuries. Its subject matter was mostly inspired by love of ancient ideals, courage and sacrifice. This translated into the production of art and architecture that reverted back to Greek and Roman themes (e.g. Doric columns and mythological stories). Its main artists were **David** and **Ingres.**

Neo-Impressionism

A development of Impressionism based on emerging scientific theories of optics and colour perception. Artists involved developed a style of painting (pointillism), using small dots of pure colour arranged side by side allowing the eye to optically mix them, thus achieving new colours. The main Neo-impressionists were **Seurat** and **Signac.**

Op Art

Derived from the Bauhaus movement, Op Art, or optical art, is concerned with the creation of optical illusions in a painting or drawing. It is sometimes called perceptual abstraction and explores the ways people understand what they see as well as how vision functions. Important artists include **Victor Vasarely, Bridget Riley, MC Escher** and the **Anonima group**, as well as **Mary Quant** in fashion.

Pop Art

Art movement of the 1950s and 1960s in which artists took their inspiration from popular culture such as comics, posters, Hollywood film and common food packaging. By using these common images, Pop artists tried to draw attention to the mundane in culture and attempted to comment upon them. Major Pop artist are **Andy Warhol, Roy Lichtenstein** and **Richard Hamilton.**

Post-Impressionism

A term first used by the British art critic Roger Fry to describe the work of a group of French artists who had rejected the ideas of Impressionism. Their dissatisfaction with what they saw to be its superficial nature caused them to become concerned with showing form, expression and structure in their work. They were to become influential in the development of art that was to follow – mainly Cubism, Expressionism and Fauvism. The main Post-Impressionists were **Cézanne, van Gogh** and **Gauguin.**

Post-Modernism

Initially a reaction to Modernism, examples of Post-modernism in art, literature and design can be seen to as early as the 1950s. The movement rejects function as the sole determiner of design and often uses elements from the past in new and unusual ways. Much Post-modernist art and design also includes elements of parody, irony and saturation, and plays with our belief in established doctrines. It can, at times, also be considered playful and quirky. Post-modernists to be aware of include **Philippe Starck, Michael Graves, Ron Arad** and **Frank Gehry.**

Pre-Raphaelites

An association of English artists formed in 1848 who shared ideas about the way art should develop. They rejected industrialization and based their ideas on the study of nature, producing detailed, carefully executed works. The main artists, whose ideas were supported by the influential art critic Ruskin included **Burne-Jones, Holman Hunt, Millais** and **Dante Rossetti.**

Realism

A nineteenth century art movement where artists painted things as they actually looked, rejecting the ideas of Neo-classicism and Romanticism. The lives of ordinary working people provided much of the inspiration for the movement. Its main artists included **Courbet, Jean-François Millet** and **Daumier.**

The Renaissance

A period of great progress in the arts, science and philosophy during the fourteenth and fifteenth centuries, mainly in Italy but also in other European countries. It was initially inspired by an interest in the arts and culture of ancient Greece and Rome. Among the main artists were **Botticelli, Donatello, Fra Angelico, Leonardo da Vinci, Michelangelo, Raphael, Titian** and **Dürer.**

Romanticism

An art movement of the early nineteenth century that emphasised the emotions, painted in a dramatic, bold style. It was a rejection of classicism and many of the works showed exotic settings in which nature was painted in a raw dramatic state. French artists included **Delacroix** and **Géricault** while British artists **Blake, Constable** and **Turner** were also seen as sharing its ideas.

Symbolism

An art movement of the late nineteenth century associated with fantasy and imagination. Symbolists were interested in mystical subjects. Their work uses visual symbols to represent ideas and themes such as our inner thoughts and feelings. Artists included **Odilon Redon, Gustav Klimt** and **Pierre Puvis de Chavannes.**

Surrealism

An art movement, associated with fantasy and imagination which started in the 1920s. Surrealists used dream-like imagery in their compositions to convey the emotion and consciousness felt in dreams. They were influenced by the psychoanalyst Sigmund Freud's ideas about the subconscious and used these in their work. Surrealist art often has odd combinations of objects set in strange settings which are painted very life-like but look unreal. Artists include **Salvador Dali, Max Ernst** and **Rene Magritte.**

Glossary

A-line	in fashion, a type of cut used in dresses and skirts that is close fitting at the top and flaring out at the bottom; shape of a dress or skirt that resembled a capital letter 'A'
Abstract	a style of work based on pure form, shape or colour that does not attempt to be a realistic representation
Abstract Expressionism	an American art movement which combined abstraction with very vigorous and expressive application of paint
Abstraction	an approach to art that does not represent reality and focuses on colour and form
Achromatic	the range of greys made using only black and white, with no other colour added
Aerial perspective	a means of showing depth or distance in a painting through the use of blue, lighter or duller hues and blurring of distant objects
Aesthetics	the rules and principles defining beauty in art
Appliqué	type of craft or design made by sticking, gluing and/or sewing various fabrics onto others for decorative effect
Assemblage	a type of three-dimensional collage, often made from found objects; typically used to describe a piece of sculpture created either as a relief or 3-dimensional
Asymmetry	a composition or arrangement that is not symmetrical i.e. evenly balanced
Atrium	in architecture, an inner space typically in the centre of a building which opens up to the whole interior space
Avant-garde	art work which is leading and ahead of its time and sometimes politically controversial
Balance	a composition in which all the elements have been deliberately arranged so that no one thing dominates
Baroque	a style of sixteenth and seventeenth century European art that is very bold and detailed; sometimes used to describe an elaborate piece of art showing movement or emotion
Bias-cut	a method of cutting fabric diagonally across the weave; achieves a very good fit to the contour of the human form
Biomorphic	2- and 3-dimensional shapes and forms that suggest animal or plant forms
Bodice	a close fitting garment for the upper body

Burnished	highly polished, typically used to refer to the surface appearance of jewellery and metalwork
Bustier	in fashion, an undergarment worn by women around the chest and just above the waist line; used by some contemporary designers as outerwear
Calibré	in jewellery, gemstones that are cut to a specific size to be fit into either rows or a setting
Cameo	a method of carving that leaves a raised, positive relief image; also refers to a carving of a person's profile set into an item of jewellery, such as a brooch
Canvas	a surface on which a painting (usually oil or acrylic) is done; made by tightly stretching a piece of canvas cloth over a wooden frame
Capital	in architecture, the top part of a column, usually carved
Caricature	usually a drawing or painting, a highly distorted likeness of something or someone; a technique often used in newspapers to exaggerate some feature of a well-known person
Cast Iron	softer metal than steel used in architecture in the nineteenth century
Chemise	a woman's undergarment; used by some designers to create interesting outerwear
Chroma	the intensity of a colour
Classical	name given to Greek art of around 500BC that was judged to be aesthetically perfect; used to indicate art influenced by those ideals
Cloisonné	in jewellery, the process of combining enamel inlay with filigree to create a decorative and colourful effect
Collage	an image or picture made by sticking together a collection of flat materials such as cloth, paper, photographs, etc.; generally 2-dimensional
Colour	what the eye sees when light is reflected off of an object; specific wavelengths of light e.g. red, yellow, blue, purple, etc.
Colour wheel	the arrangements of colours in a circle to represent the spectrum
Complementary colours	colours that are directly opposite each other on the colour wheel i.e. the primary colour red and the secondary colour green, made from mixing the two remaining primary colours
Composition	how the elements of a picture are put together
Conceptual art	an art form mainly concerned with expressing an idea or concept; does not value the artistic product in itself, such as a painting or piece of sculpture
Constructivism	an early twentieth century art movement that focused on making art using non-traditional materials; its output was mostly sculpture constructed with materials such as steel, glass or plastics
Contour drawing	a line drawing that follows the edge of an object
Decadence	art that is considered to be only about surface and form without any real depth of meaning or content
Degenerate art	a term of abuse used by Nazi Germany to describe early twentieth century modern art
Dominance	an element that is the primary focus or stands out in a composition or design
Drape	a cloth that is hung as a background to a model in a drawing or painting; also refers to the way fabric hangs in a garment

Egg tempera	a medium for painting composed of pigment and egg yolk; usually used to paint on a hard gesso surface
Embossed	a raised surface decoration
Embroidery	ornamental needlework used to add intricate surface decoration to fabric
Empire	a design style popular during the period when Napoleon was emperor of France; characterised by a high waist that sits just below the bust line
Encaustic	a form of painting using coloured, hot liquid wax; a technique used by the ancient Greek and Romans
Engrave	cutting into a flat surface to make a picture or design; *see also relief and intaglio*
Etching	a form of intaglio printing where the lines are not cut, but 'etched' with acid into the surface of a printing plate
Ethnic	in fashion, clothing inspired by the traditional costumes of various nations
Façade	the front of a building
Faux	false or imitation; used to describe design work where less expensive materials are substituted for the real thing
Filigree	a very fine, intricately detailed design usually made of twisted strands of fine wire and set into a frame of stronger wire; used with enamel to create cloisonné work
Fishtail (train)	a skirt or dress that is fitted around the hips of the body and flares out considerably at the bottom
Form	one of the visual elements; 3-dimensional shape e.g. a circle is a shape whereas a sphere is a form
Found object	artwork created with objects the artist has found and incorporated into the composition without much alteration
Fresco	a painting carried out directly onto the surface of a wall or ceiling while the plaster is still damp, allowing the pigment to sink into it and become permanent
Frottage	another word for a 'rubbing'; a piece of paper or canvas laid over a textured surface and rubbed with a pencil or crayon to pick up the underlying design
Gelatine silver	a process used in photography to create black and white images; paper coated with a layer of gelatine and silver salts that does not fade or yellow over time
Genre	categories of art such as history, mythology, religion, portraiture, landscape and still life
Gestural	very loosely handled drawing or painting where the artist has used energetic sweeping marks to suggest movement and form
Glaze	a transparent layer of colour, usually over opaque paint; if glazes are applied over each other, great depth and luminosity can be achieved
Gouache	an opaque watercolour paint
Hatching	the use of parallel lines in a drawing to suggest tone; crossing these lines in another direction gives darker tones and is called cross-hatching

Haute Couture	high fashion; the latest styles
Highlight	the most brightly lit parts of an image or object
Hue	a specific shade of colour
Hyper-realism	a very precise form of realism which looks almost photographic
Impasto	the thickness of paint on a picture; very thick, lumpy paint may be described as being 'heavy impasto'
Inlay	the placing of a material, such as metal or enamel, flush into a surface to create a design
Installation	art work which is set or installed in a location; usually combines different media and materials and may include sculpture, moving images and sound
Intaglio	a method of carving an image into a substance as a negative; the opposite of cameo; used in printing and to make raised seals
Intensity	the strength of a colour
Intermediate colours	the variations in between primary and secondary colours in the colour wheel e.g. red-orange or fuchsia
Jersey	soft knitted fabric made fashionable by Coco Chanel
Kinetic	a branch of sculpture whereby parts of the sculpture move, either naturally by wind or water, or mechanically through a motor
Kitsch	art which is in bad taste and poor quality, overly slick and/or pretentious
Land art	works made by artists in the landscape using natural, found materials such as earth, leaves, stones etc.
Landscape	a work of art that depicts scenery
Line	one of the visual elements; delineates space and contour on a page; an angle or shape in a design
Linocut	a form of printing where an image is printed from the surface of a piece of lino; negative areas of the print are cut from the surface, which is then inked and pressed against paper
Lithograph	an image created and reproduced by lightly etching a metal plate or stone, coating it with ink and pressing it against paper
Mechanical Art	art that uses elements of mechanical construction for its creation
Media	various materials used to make a work of art; the plural of medium
Medium	materials used to create a work of art e.g. paint, ink pencil etc.
Minimalism	an art movement of the 1960s where artists worked with basic geometric shapes, simple forms and large areas of colour with little realistic content
Mixed media	an art work made from a varied range of materials
Monochrome	tones of a single colour
Mural	a painting executed on a wall

Narrative	an artwork or design that tells a story
Naturalism	a style of painting that shows nature exactly as it is
Natural waist	on a human body, the narrowest part of the midriff
Neutral	colour that is earthy, brown or grey
Op art	a mid twentieth century art movement where the artist attempted to create optical sensations in the viewer
Orientalist	an artist or designer who finds inspiration in the art of the Far East
Organic	art created with shapes and contours that resemble those found in the natural world; artwork created using materials that are naturally occurring
Palette	the tray on which an artist lays out colours; a range of colours used in a particular painting by an artist
Pastel	pigments pressed into a chalk or crayon-like form; used for drawing
Perspective	an approach to representing 3-dimensional objects in depth on a flat surface
Pieced	creation of an item or work of art by joining smaller elements together; in fashion, creating a garment by sewing together many elements, such as patchwork
Pigment	a coloured substance that, when mixed with a binder, becomes a paint or colouring material
Pixellated	art work that resembles a computer image made up of pixels, or tiny shapes of colour
Plane	a flat or level surface; visually flat surfaces within an artwork
Pleat	a fold in fabric/cloth; created by doubling the material back onto itself and pressing or stitching it into place
Plein Air	painting out of doors in the open air; an approach used by the Impressionists
Pointillism	a way of painting with dots of pure colour so that when seen from a distance they appear to mix; also called optical mixing
Polyester	man made fibre which was important in the evolution of fashion in the twentieth century
Prêt-a-porter	fashion items that are ready to wear, off the shelf
Primary colours	colours that cannot be made by mixing other colours i.e. red, yellow, and blue
Primitivism	an approach to art that celebrates basic human existence and actions; focuses on the simplicity of life and rejects modernisation
Process Art	an artistic movement that focuses on the process of creating art rather than the end result; an exploration in creativity and action
Proportion	the relative size of one thing compared to another
Purism	a form of cubism that emphasised a return to basic forms; also inspired by machinery
Rayon	man made fibre important in the development of fashion
Ready-made	art created with everyday items, often which have been mass-produced; term first coined by Marcel Duchamp; *see also found object*

Realism	a nineteenth century art movement which concentrated on showing scenes from everyday life; any art which concentrates on depicting the real world as it is seen
Relief	a sculpture or carving that projects from a surface; a positive, raised image
Repetition	term used in design when a feature is repeated to give an ordered effect
Representational	art where recognisable objects, people and places are shown realistically
Rhythm	using colour, shape or line to create a flowing harmonious effect
Secondary colours	colours made by mixing a pair of primary colours e.g. red and blue make the secondary colour purple
Screenprint	a type of printing where a stencil is attached to a fine-mesh covered frame; the printing ink is pushed through the mesh, only reaching the areas not covered by the stencil
Shade	a colour mixed with black to change its tone
Spectrum	the range of colours achieved by projecting white light through a prism e.g. red, orange, yellow, etc.
Symmetry	the exact balance of shapes or parts on either side of a straight line or plane
Tempera	a water based paint that uses a binder to make it stable
Tertiary colours	colour made by mixing two secondary colours, or by mixing a primary colour with either of the colours adjacent to it on the colour wheel e.g. combining green and orange, or red with orange or purple
Texture	the roughness or smoothness of a surface
Tint	the shades of a colour when mixed with different amounts of white
Tone	the variations in a colour; *see also value*
Traditional	art that follows established doctrines and uses techniques passed down through generations
Triptych	a picture composed on three separate panels
Underpainting	the first layer of paint on a surface; often used to establish the basic tones of a composition and thereafter is overprinted with colours of the appropriate value
Value	the brightness or darkness of a colour; also called tonal value
Vintage	relating to fashion, an item that represents a particular period of time or era e.g. 1950s
Wash	a very thin layer of paint typically used as a base or finish to a watercolour painting
Watercolour	a semi-transparent painting medium composed of fine pigments and a binder, such as gum or glycerine; used by mixing with small amounts of water; usually applied to paper

Illustrations

43   *Still Life with Fruit*, MMV Art Limited/Douglas Muego

44   *Fruits of the Midi* © Francis G. Mayer/CORBIS

45   *Still Life with Basket* © The Gallery Collection/Corbis

45   *Irises*, Van Gogh Museum, Amsterdam, The Netherlands/ Roger-Viollet, Paris/The Bridgeman Art Library

46   *Still Life Before an Open Window* © 2008 Artists Rights Society (ARS), New York/ADAGP, Paris. Photo © Burstein Collection/CORBIS

46   *Still Life* © Succession Picasso/DACS 2008, Photo © Tate, London

47   *Goldfish and Sculpture* © Succession H Matisse/ DACS 2008, Photo © The Museum of Modern Art, New York/Scala, Florence

47   *The Studio* © ADAGP, Paris and DACS, London 2008 Photo © 2007, Image copyright © The Museum of Modern Art, New York/Art Resource/Scala, Florence

48   *Sandwich and Soda* © The Estate of Roy Lichtenstein/DACS 2008, Photo: Fred Jones Jr. Museum of Art, University of Oklahoma, USA/Alumni Development Fund, Estate of Roy Lichtenstein/The Bridgeman Art Library

48   *Tulips*, Tate, London 2008

48   *Still Life* © ADAGP, Paris and DACS, London 2008, © Photo CNAC/MNAM Dist. RMN - Jaqueline Hyde

48   *Pepper No 30*, Collection Center for Creative Photography, © 1981 Arizona Board of Regents

49   *Still Life with Vermillion Vase and Yellow Tile* © The artist's estate, Photo © Christie's Images Limited

49   *Two Cats with Clivia* © Elizabeth Blackadder, © Christie's Images Limited

54   *The Agony in the Garden*, National Gallery, London, UK/The Bridgeman Art Library

55   *The Great Piece of Lawn (The Large Turf)*, akg-images

55   *Wivenhoe Park*, National Gallery of Art, Washington DC, USA/The Bridgeman Art Library

56   *Rainbow, Pontoise*, akg-images

56   *The Solitary Tree*, akg-images

57   *Snow Storm – Steam-Boat off a Harbour's Mouth* © AKG London/Erich Lessing

58   *A Regatta on the Grand Canal* © National Gallery Collection; By kind permission of the Trustees of the National Gallery, London/CORBIS

58   *Dance of the Nymphs*, akg-images/Erich Lessing

59   *In Glen Massan*, Glasgow City Council (Museums)

60   *The Water-Lily Pond* © National Gallery Collection; By kind permission of the Trustees of the National Gallery, London/CORBIS

61   *The Bay at Marselles, Seen from L'Estaque*, Photography © The Art Institute of Chicago

62   *Wheatfield with Cypresses* © The London Art Archive/Alamy

62, 73   *Viaduct at L'Estaque* © ADAGP, Paris and DACS, London 2008, Photo: The Art Archive/Musée National d'art moderne Paris/Gianni Dagli Orti

62   *Landscape with a Bridge*, © Succession Picasso/DACS 2008, Photo © National Gallery in Prague 200

63   *North Wind, Iona*, The Bridgeman Art Library

63   *The Village of Lagonne*, Glasgow City Council (Museums)

63   *Geological Landscape* © Estate of Prunella Clough 2008. All Rights Reserved DACS, Photo: Tate, London 2008

64   *Juniper, Lake Tenya*, Center for Creative Photography, © Arizona Board of Regents. Photo: National Gallery of Canada, Ottawa

64   *Mount Clarence King, Pool, Kings Canyon National Park, California* © Ansel Adams Publishing Rights Trust/CORBIS

65   *Spiral Jetty* © Estate of Robert Smithson/DACS, London/VAGA, New York 2008, Photo © George Steinmetz/Corbis

65   *Surrounding Islands* © Christo, Photo © Bettmann/ CORBIS

65   Andy Goldsworthy

71   *The Trongate*, Glasgow City Council (Museums)

72   *Moret-sur-Loing*, The Bridgeman Art Library

72   *Gardanne* © The Barnes Foundation, Merion Station, Pennsylvania/CORBIS

73   *St Paul's from the Thames* © ADAGP, Paris and DACS, London 2008, Photo: Minneapolis Institute of Arts, Bequest of Putnam Dana McMillan

74   *Champ de Mars: The Red Tower* © L & M Services B.V. The Hague 20080906, Photo © The Art Institute of Chicago

74   *Nighthawks*, Photograph by Robert Hashimoto/ Reproduction, The Art Institute of Chicago

75   *Evening, North Berwick*, Glasgow City Council (Museums)

75   *Place Furstenburg, Paris: August 7, 8 & 9, 1985* © DAVID HOCKNEY

76   Whiteread House© Ian Goodrick/Alamy

77   Sculptures, Photography © Elizabeth Hayes

80   Roxy Paine *Scumak No. 2*, 2001 aluminum, computer, conveyor, electronics, extruder, stainless steel, polyethylene, Teflon © Roxy Paine, image courtesy of James Cohan Gallery, New York

80   *The Thousand and One Nights in the Mansion of Bliss*, Kunstmuseum Luzern/Courtesy of Alice Aycock

81   *St George and the Dragon* © National Gallery Collection; By kind permission of the Trustees of the National Gallery, London/CORBIS

81,84   *The Cyclops* © The London Art Archive/Alamy

81   *Temptation of St Anthony* © ADAGP, Paris and DACS, London 2008, Photo: Wilhelm Lehmbruck Museum, Duisberg, Germany/The Bridgeman Art Library

133, 153 Casa Battlo © Marion Kaplan/Alamy
134 Robie House © Farrell Grehan/CORBIS
134 Mackintosh Room at The Glasgow School of Art, image courtesy of The Glasgow School of Art 1990
135 Library at The Glasgow School of Art (1909), image courtesy of Glasgow School of Art 1992
136 Wassily chair © Elizabeth Whiting & Associates/Alamy
136 'Barcelona' Model MR90 chair, Museum of Fine Arts, Houston, Texas, USA/ Museum purchase with funds from by J. Brian and Varina Eby/The Bridgeman Art Library
137 Schroeder House, The Bridgeman Art Library
137 Hotel Solvay, akg-images/Hilbich
137 Sideboard © Philadelphia Museum of Art/CORBIS
137 Ivory side table, DEA/A. DAGLIORTI/De Agostini Picture Library/Getty Images
138 Pompidou Centre © Ian Dagnall/Alamy
138 The Royalton Hotel © Arcaid/Alamy
140, 146 Exterior of The Glasgow School of Art, image courtesy of The Glasgow School of Art/Eric Thorburn 2002
141 Science Centre and BBC Waterfront, courtesy of The Glasgow School of Art,'Glasgow: Past, Present and Future' Exhibition, McLellan Galleries, 2007
141 Bus shelter, image © Heather MacNeill 2008
142 Falling Water © Richard A. Cooke/CORBIS
142 Lloyds Building © Hoberman Collection UK/Alamy
142 Hong Kong and Shanghai Bank © Martin Jones; Ecoscene/CORBIS
143, 160 Guggenheim Museum, Bilbao © Rolf Haid/dpa/Corbis
144 Atrium of the Hong Kong and Shanghai Bank © Bernd Mellmann/Alamy
145 Casa Battlo © scenicireland.com /Christopher Hill Photographic/Alamy
145 Art Nouveau detail of The Glasgow School of Art, image excerpt courtesy of The Glasgow School of Art/Alan McAteer 2003
145 Chiat/Day Mojo Advertising Agency © Rodolfo Arpia/Alamy
146 The Glasgow School of Art alternative view, image courtesy of The Glasgow School of Art/Eric Thorburn 2003
147 The Parthenon © Art Kowalsky/Alamy
147 Church on the Hill, Glasgow, image © Heather MacNeill 2008
147 National Gallery of Art, London, image © Heather MacNeill 2008
147 Paisley Town Hall, image © Heather MacNeill 2008
147 Cumberland Terrace, London © Kim Sayer/CORBIS
148 Entablature of Classical architecture, image © Heather MacNeill 2008
148 Close-ups of St Vincent Street Church, images © Heather MacNeill 2008

148 Flying buttress image © Heather MacNeill 2008
148 Rib vaulting image © Heather MacNeill 2008
149 St Pancras Station, London, image © Heather MacNeill 2008
149 The Houses of Parliament, London, image © Heather MacNeill 2008
150 Eiffel Tower, image © Elizabeth Hayes 2008
150 Crystal Palace, London © V&A Images
150 Wainwright Building © ART on FILE/CORBIS
151 The Red House © Arcaid/Alamy
153 Sagrada Familia © G P Bowater/Alamy
154 Chrysler Building, NYC © Jon Arnold Images Ltd/Alamy
155 Seagram Building NYC © Philip Scalia/Alamy
157 Villa Savoye © Edifice/The Bridgeman Art Library
157 SECC, Glasgow, image © Heather MacNeill 2008
157 Humana Building © Wm. Baker/GhostWorx Images/Alamy
160 Phaeno Science Centre, DPA/PA Photos
165 Knox pendant © V&A Images
165 Ashbee brooch © V&A Images/Printed with kind permission of Francis Ames-Lewis
167, 171 Lalique corsage © ADAGP, Paris and DACS, London 2008. Photo: Calouste Gulbenkian Foundation
167 Dragonfly brooch (A1999.37) Copyright Tiffany & Co. Archives 2008. (Not to be published or reproduced without prior permission.)
168 Fouquet brooch © ADAGP, Paris and DACS, London 2008. Photo © V&A Images
170 Templier brooch © V&A Images
171 Chang brooch, Printed with permission of Peter Chang © V&A Images
172 Journey narrative brooch, Jack Cunningham
174 Evening dress © V&A Images
177 Fancy dress costume © 2008, Image copyright The Metropolitan Museum of Art/Art Resource/Scala, Florence
178 Chanel, Sasha/Getty Images
179 Fortuny evening dress © V&A Images
179 Vionnet gowns © 2007, Image copyright The Metropolitan Museum of Art/Art Resource/Scala, Florence
180 Elsa Schiaparelli dresses © V&A Images
181 Dior's New Look, Topfoto.co.uk
182 Mary Quant dress © V&A Images
184 Vivienne Westwood collection © Benoit Tessier/Reuters/Corbis
184 Hamnett collection, Scott Barbour/Getty Images
185 Issey Miyake collection © Pierre Vauthey/CORBIS SYGMA
186 Christian Dior collection © Condé Nast Archive/Corbis
186 Alexander McQueen collection © Benoit Tessier/Reuters/Corbis
180 Ferragamo sandal © V&A Images

Index